D0250485

intimate conversations

DEVOTIONS *to* NURTURE *a* WOMAN'S SOUL

alicia britt chole

Revell

a division of Baker Publishing Group
Grand Rapids, Michigan

© 2009 by Alicia Britt Chole

Published by Revell
a division of Baker Publishing Group
P.O. Box 6287, Grand Rapids, MI 49516-6287
www.revellbooks.com

Printed in the United States of America

All rights reserved. No part of this publication may be reproduced, stored in a retrieval system, or transmitted in any form or by any means—for example, electronic, photocopy, recording—without the prior written permission of the publisher. The only exception is brief quotations in printed reviews.

Library of Congress Cataloging-in-Publication Data
Chole, Alicia Britt.
    Intimate conversations : devotions to nurture a woman's soul / Alicia Britt Chole.
        p.   cm.
    Includes bibliographical references.
    ISBN 978-0-8007-3289-9 (pbk.)
    1. Mothers—Prayers and devotions. 2. Christian women—Prayers and devo-
tions. I. Title.
BV4847.C49 2009
252'.6431—dc22   2009014450

Unless otherwise indicated, Scripture is taken from the HOLY BIBLE, NEW INTER-
NATIONAL VERSION®. NIV®. Copyright © 1973, 1978, 1984 by International Bible
Society. Used by permission of Zondervan. All rights reserved.

Scripture marked NKJV is taken from the New King James Version. Copyright © 1982
by Thomas Nelson, Inc. Used by permission. All rights reserved.

Published in association with the literary agency of Alive Communications, Inc., 7680
Goddard Street, Suite 200, Colorado Springs, Colorado 80920. www.alivecommunica
tions.com

intimate
conversations

To Angie Britt, my incredible mom.
Thank you for celebrating all of my scribbles, from my first wobbly sentence to my most recent book.
You are the most generous soul I have ever known.
Te quiero, mama.

Contents

Dear God . . . Why Do I Feel So Unproductive?

Dear God . . . The Grass Is *Really* Looking Greener Elsewhere

Dear God . . . Today My Faith Feels Frail

Dear God . . . I'm Not Sure That I Can Keep Going

Dear God . . . I'm Withdrawing and I Don't Know Why

Dear God . . . Why Do Those Who Love You Suffer?

Dear God . . . Help Me See as You See

Dear God . . . Please Refresh My Love for You

Dear God . . . Grant Me Wisdom for This Journey

Foreword

I first met Alicia Chole backstage at a women's conference in Minnesota where we were both to speak. From that time on, we have shared many cups of tea, great conversation, and friendship.

Let me introduce you to the Alicia I love—she will become your friend too as you read the pages of this book.

I like to think of people as if they were colors. I do this because I am blind and can't see them to form a visual image, but I find even sighted people can see what I perceive when I describe a person as if they were a color. So, if you've never met my multicolored friend Alicia Chole, let me introduce you to her by showing you the colors I see.

Alicia is *sage*. Sage is the grayish green color of sage leaves. Either fresh or dry, the leaves are used aromatically as seasoning. Sage is also defined as having wisdom that comes from age and experience. A person who bears the title "Sage" is a mentor in spiritual topics and is characterized by profound wisdom.

Sage is definitely one of the colors of Alicia because she is warm, aromatic, wise, and willing to lead others to wisdom. The green hue of Alicia's sage is that of the pastures which the good shepherd leads us to lie in. Her soul bears the color of peace. But in certain light, I can see the color gray more prominently—it's the tint of thoughts churning and honest deliberation. Whether gray shows up more on some days or lots of green is primary on others, the well-seasoned color sage is the color of Alicia. It's the color of wisdom and spice, depth and experience. In the coming pages, you may read black print on white paper, but you will certainly see the color sage because Alicia has allowed what God has written upon her life to be wisely written in this book.

Alicia is *terra-cotta*. Terra-cotta is the distinctive orangey, brownish, and rust color of ceramic clay. What makes terra-cotta so unique and lovely is that it gains its deep and rich intensity from exposure to the elements. It's out there.

Just like Alicia, terra-cotta doesn't gain its beauty from the shadowed protection of tidy safety. It gains its rich hue from the wind, weather, and sun. Alicia's soft and open soul is terra-cotta because she has allowed herself to be touched, tenderized, and toughened by the world she lives in. I think you will really like it when you see this color in her writing. But, she's also terra-cotta to me because she is earthy! I always kid her when we go to the coffee shop together, "I hope they have tea earthy enough for you; if not, we'll bring a shovel and you can drink some fresh-brewed dirt and grass!" It's not far from true. Her poetic and practical style reflects the warm and organic hue of orangey, rusty brown that will warm you. When your eye catches a tinge of terra-cotta as you read, you will say, "She knows how I feel" or "I've thought that same thing." In these pages, you'll see the rich, inviting color of life well lived.

Alicia is *ruby red*. Ruby red is one of the most intense hues in the spectrum of the color red. It's dazzling, eye catching, and captivating. Rubies have always been held in high esteem. They were historically used to ornament armor, scabbards, and harnesses of noblemen in China and India. Rubies were even laid beneath foundations of buildings because it was believed that rubies at the base would secure good fortune to the structure.

12

Why do I see Alicia as ruby red? It is because she has an intensity that's attractive; she's dazzling and highly esteemed. But mostly it's because down deep, beneath that warm, tender, and wise woman is a girl with some sassiness and pizzazz! Just like a subtle sprinkle of cinnamon on your coffee, a bright red cherry on your sundae, or a dazzling red balloon at your birthday party, Alicia gives you that extra zing that makes you smile. She does it with wit and a whimsical way of looking at life. You'll see little splashes of ruby red as you take this devotional journey; and when you glimpse it, you'll smile and thank God for how good life can be!

Alicia Britt Chole is uniquely qualified to offer a book called *Intimate Conversations* because I know for a fact that she engages in intimate conversations with her heavenly Father every day, and it has made her life beautifully colored with the shade of his grace.

Oh, I know you will love *Intimate Conversations*, I sure do. I challenge you to answer the questions at the end of each devotional, for the truths they reveal will bring out the colors of your soul. You too will reflect the lovely and subtle shades of his grace, wisdom, and love that come only from spending intimate time in conversation with the beautiful one.

Pour yourself a cup of tea—one that has more flavor than dirt—and spend some time letting my friend Alicia provide a charming place for you to gain a deeper friendship with your heavenly Father. Her colorful life has done that for me, and I know her words along with God's Word will color your life with richness.

So, enjoy!

Jennifer Rothschild
author of *Lessons I Learned in the Dark*
and *Self Talk, Soul Talk*
www.jenniferrothschild.com

Dear God . . .

I Ache

to Know You More

Uh-

Good morning, God, I'm so gra— (excuse me, God).
"You can have a snack after lunch."
I'm so grateful for th— (just a second, God). "Your
shoes are in the laundry room."
**I'm so grateful for this time we ha— (sorry for the
interruption, God).** "They're there. Moooove things."
**I'm so grateful for the time we have together to—
(God, I think we'll have to continue this lat—).**
"No, you are not old enough to change baby's poopy
diaper. I'M COMING!"

Complete sentences. What a luxury.

This was one of the first things my friends commented on when I suddenly became a mother through the miracle of adoption at the age of thirty-one. We used to spend hours talking each week about the great mysteries of life. I was a highly focused conversationalist—a sincere listener who was rarely distracted.

Now? Well, I am still a sincere listener—I am continually listening for the sounds and (of greater concern) the non-sounds of my three children whenever I am on the phone. Frankly, I think I miss half of what my friends say and it can take minutes to complete a single sentence *if* I do not forget what it was we were talking about in the first place.

In addition to giving me more empathy for those who live with attention-deficit disorders, this new chronically interrupted era of life has provided an opportunity for me to reconsider how I nurture relationships— with my husband, with my children, with my friends, and especially with my God.

Specifically, the new era revealed a weakness: I was too dependent on shared words, on well-formed sentences, on neat and tidy blocks of time.

The last dozen years have affirmed an encouraging reality: intimacy with God is not on hold, waiting for me to control my environment and carve out serene aromatic spaces. Intimacy with God is not on pause until I can complete sentences and listen without interruptions.

Each minute of every loud, distracting day is pregnant with potential for intimacy if I can simply and intentionally live it *with* God.

Being *with* God was—and still is—the first priority of a disciple's job description:

> *Jesus went up on a mountainside and called to him those he wanted, and they came to him. He appointed twelve— designating them apostles—that they might be with him and that he might send them out to preach and to have authority to drive out demons.*
>
> *Mark 3:13–15*

The Gospels record Jesus' conversations and teachings. However, the printed page cannot convey what a 24/7 camera would have captured. Most of Jesus' three years with the disciples was spent not in deep ponderings but in daily proximity. They simply experienced life side by side, walking together, sitting together, working together, and consciously being near one another.

Right now, this same Jesus is *with* us. With or without interruptions. With or without words.

As we awaken each morning, God issues us a personal invitation to intimacy.

(RSVP desired.)

For Discussion and Reflective Journaling

I am always with you.
Psalm 73:23

One. In this season of your life, how much can you relate to this devotional's starting prayer?

Two. What adjectives would you use to describe your structured devotional life?

Three. Jesus certainly set the example of private prayer times. But he also set an example that is less quantifiable: he consciously lived each moment connected to, and aware of, his Father God. Spend a few minutes meditating on the following statements that Jesus made:

> *If anyone loves me, he will obey my teaching. My Father will love him, and we will come to him and make our home with him.*
> *John 14:23*

> *Remain in me, and I will remain in you.*
> *John 15:4*

> *As the Father has loved me, so have I loved you. Now remain in my love.*
> *John 15:9*

Four. Consider the point made in the devotional about how Jesus and his disciples spent the majority of their time together. Make a conscious effort today to "see" Jesus with you, near you, in your daily life. Remember that he is with you while you are making your bed. Gratefully acknowledge his presence while you respond to an email. Smile at him as you are stuck in traffic.

Then throughout this coming week, intentionally increase your awareness that God is *with* you (and he is happy about it!).

19

Everything

For decades I have prayed that somehow God would allow me to know him as Brother Lawrence knew him—moment by moment. *The Practice of the Presence of God* is one of the most well-loved and well-worn books in my home. On one of its discolored pages, Brother Lawrence penned sentences that haunt me:

> People seek for methods of learning to love God . . . Is it not much shorter and more direct to do everything for the love of God . . . ?[1]

Every-thing for the love of God.
Every-*thing* for the love of God.

Brother Lawrence goes on to say,

> In the way of God, thoughts count for little, love does everything. And it is not necessary to have great things to do. I turn my little omelet in the pan for the love of God; when it is finished, if I have nothing to do, I prostrate myself on the ground and adore my God, who gave me the grace to make it, after which I arise, more content than a king.[2]

Brother Lawrence was a monk in a monastery. I am a mother in Missouri. So what does "everything for the love of God" look like for me?

Today I . . .

changed my baby's diaper . . . for the love of God
picked up the family room . . . for the love of God
mediated a sibling dispute . . . for the love of God
hugged my beloved husband . . . for the love of God
set up a lunch with a young writer . . . for the love of God
paid a bill . . . for the love of God
put away dishes . . . for the love of God
wiped milk off the floor . . . for the love of God
gave away a book . . . for the love of God
wrote this devotional . . . for the love of God

God accepted each act as worship! And tomorrow I hope to
remember him more . . . *everything* for the love of God.

For Discussion and Reflective Journaling

**And whatever you do, whether in word or deed, do
it all in the name of the Lord Jesus, giving thanks to
God the Father through him.**
Colossians 3:17

One. Picture Brother Lawrence turning an omelet at the monastery
for the love of God. Now picture yourself turning an omelet in your
kitchen for the love of God. The monastery did not make the act into
an offering of spiritual intimacy—Brother Lawrence's attitude did.

Two. Make a list of the small things you must do today. What
would it be like to do them "for the love of God"?

Three. This principle opened up to me a world of new opportunities
to develop intimacy with God. What changes might you experience
as a result of integrating this attitude deeper into your life?

Cuddle Time

When our eldest transitioned to a "big" bed, we began a treasured tradition called *cuddle time*. After the last bathroom stop, after the toothbrush is rinsed, after we pray and sing "Jesus Loves Me," we simply cuddle and enjoy being together.

My husband and I both work from home—we enjoy the kids' company all day long. But this time at night is still special, unique, and protected. The kids consider this space sacred.

Lest anyone think that being quiet and still is natural for my kids, allow me to share that visitors have a hard time believing we have only three children because it sounds, and feels, like we have six. I am quiet but my kids are LOUD. I enjoy stillness but my kids are VERY active.

Except during cuddle time.

Then Jonathan softly asks me penetrating questions. Keona dreams with me about her future plans. Preverbal Louie offers me his favorite car and looks deeply into my eyes. When words cease, Jonathan tries to hear my heartbeat. Keona asks me to scratch her back. Louie stays perfectly still, not wanting the moment to end.

This is cuddle time. This is one of the precious, priceless jewels in my mommy-heart.

As I give one more kiss and walk out the bedroom door, I am often reminded that God's daddy-heart treasures such times with me. He longs for me to curl up in a chair and rest with him. He waits for me to softly ask penetrating questions and listen for his heartbeat. He hopes that I will offer him my physical treasures and look deeply into his eyes.

My kids may someday "outgrow" cuddle time with me. But I pray that none of us ever outgrow cuddle time with Father God.

For Discussion and Reflective Journaling

He took a little child and had him stand among them. Taking him in his arms, he said to them, "Whoever welcomes one of these little children in my name welcomes me; and whoever welcomes me does not welcome me but the one who sent me."
Mark 9:36–37

One. Nothing can quite touch the experience of a child falling asleep in your embrace. What adjectives would you use to describe how you feel when a child sinks into your arms and drifts off to sleep?

Two. Take those adjectives and use them to describe how Father God feels when you rest in him: "When I become still and lean on God, he feels _____."

Three. Tonight, before going to bed, try to carve out a few minutes to become still enough, long enough, alone enough to sigh and whisper, "Father, I love you."

Fresh Ink

Fresh ink was on my Day-Timer. A glass of cool water sat on my desk. My fingers were dancing across the keyboard when I heard Father God whisper in my soul:

> *"Child, walk with me. The day is new and my heart longs for you."*

My fingers paused as I hesitated. Withdrawing from the swift current of that day's "to-do" list—as a wife, mother, speaker, and mentor—was like resisting gravity. Closing my eyes, I recalled the countless lost promises of "Soon, Father God, soon." Turning from the ocean of undone, I took his offered hand.

The wet grass soaked the bottom of my pant legs, and we began walking together. The silence we shared was like breathing pure life. Then he spoke again:

> *"Child, am I your Love or your business partner? You seem to find more value in being busy than in simply being."*

"But, Father God," I countered, "in the world, even in the church, busyness is a sign of commitment."

> *"Yes, child. But commitment to whom? Commitment to what?"*

I began to think: Why am I so busy? When did I begin to find value in a full schedule? What motivates my "yes" to task and to people?

I began to study: The voice of need always cried out to Jesus, yet he never seemed hurried, stressed, or driven. He disappointed many people to stay true to the purpose of his Father.

Then I dared to ask: I am busy, but am I fruitful?

And so a new chapter in my spiritual journey began. "Less busy, more fruitful" became my mantra. "Simplify and focus" became my means.

That conversation took place long ago. Looking back, I now realize that Father's words not only simplified my life, they saved my life.

For Discussion and Reflective Journaling

Be still, and know that I am God.
Psalm 46:10

One. Survey your initial response to the dialogue above. What words, phrases, concepts capture your interest?

Two. If someone unfamiliar with God were to describe—from observation alone—your relationship with God, what words might he or she select? God is your . . . Co-worker? Love? Coach? Critic? Friend? Santa Claus? Life? Source? Other?

Three. Does your schedule seem livable? If you could change three things about your schedule and pace of living, what would you select? Why?

Four. What would it cost—in time, money, favor, future—to make these three changes?

Five. What will it cost—in heart, spirit, health, vision, family, eternity—not to make these changes?

Dear God . . .

Grow Something
Good in My Soul

While Stirring the Oatmeal

"Why did the snow leopard turn out to be evil, Mom?" five-year-old Keona asked with a worried tone.

Turning off the oatmeal on the stove, I picked up a pad of paper and a pen to settle into a mentoring moment with Daddy's princess. Most of these opportunities are unexpected, but I saw this one coming the first time we cuddled together as a family to watch the new movie one Friday night.

An infant was placed on the doorstep of a good man, a kung fu master, who "raised the child as his own." But the baby boy grew to be a powerful, evil warrior.

Amidst the humor and excellent animation, a disturbing question arose for my children: How can someone with "good" parents grow to become a "bad" person? As adults, the answer is sobering: choice is a destiny shaper. As children, though, the answer can be paralyzing.

So I responded with pictures. Drawing a tree from the trunk up, I said, "Keona, Mommy is drawing a tree filled with fruit. What kind of fruit tree do you want it to be?"

"An orange tree!" she said with wide eyes. "But, Mommy, you forgot the roots."

"That's on purpose, babe. Here, first help me fill the tree with fruit." When our tree was loaded with oranges, I drew two small roots at the bottom and asked, "What would happen if a tree with all this fruit only had two short, little roots?"

"It would fall down," she said quickly.

29

"You're right. In fact, underground, roots are two to three times broader than the tree branches," I continued as I drew out the roots that would be needed to support such a fruit-laden tree.

Labeling the tree, I said, "Well, in my illustration: *fruit* equal *giftings* and *roots* equal *virtue*. The snow leopard had many gifts. He was fast, smart, and skilled at kung fu. But he spent more time developing his giftings than developing virtues like love, joy, peace, patience, kindness, goodness, faithfulness, gentleness, and self-control. So what happened to his life?"

"It fell down," Keona replied, staring at the drawing. Then she looked into my eyes and her brow relaxed. I could see it in her eyes: our outrageously gifted daughter understood why we place such emphasis on virtue in our family.

"Can I have maple syrup in my oatmeal?" she inquired, without missing a beat. "Yes, my love," I replied, turning on the stove once again. But lest I wonder if the lesson was heard, dear Keona said softly to herself, "I'll keep this tree picture in my journal."

P.S. It was some of the best oatmeal we have ever shared.

For Discussion and Reflective Journaling

A farmer went out to sow his seed. . . . Some fell on rocky places, where it did not have much soil. It sprang up quickly, because the soil was shallow. But when the sun came up, the plants were scorched, and they withered because they had no root.

Matthew 13:3, 5–6

One. Nature, nurture, and free will are at the heart of an age-old debate. Review your own childhood and identify (1) one strength you inherited from your family, (2) one weakness you did *not* inherit from your family, and (3) one personal choice that is utterly unique in your family.

Two. Reflect on the orange tree illustration. Whether or not you feel laden with fruit, what adjectives would you use to describe your root system (for example, shallow, deep, narrow, broad, thin, thick, vulnerable, hearty, etc.)?

Three. Reflect on the fate of the second seed in Jesus' parable from Matthew 13:3, 5–6. Contrast the difference between what people saw above ground and what was really happening below ground.

Four. Conclude in prayer with gratitude to your loving God who values the unseen growth of virtue in your life above the public display of talents.

Every Choice Is a Seed

Choices: we make them all day long.
We make choices through . . .

deliberate decision: "I have decided!"

passive postponement: "I'll decide . . . later. God, I'll say 'yes' tomorrow" (which is really a choice to say "no" today).

the deception of denial: "It's not a problem. Everything is just fine."

Whether made through deliberate decision, passive postponement, or the deception of denial, all of our choices do one thing: every choice plants a seed.

Picture your spirit as though it were a garden. Day after day, choice after choice, every choice is a seed and, in the realm of choice, *every* seed bears fruit.

How is your garden growing?

We are a generation living on the edge of unimaginable change politically, economically, environmentally, and spiritually. At such a time as this, when much seems *out of* our control, we must be accountable for what is *within* our control. We must be a generation that takes responsibility for all our choices.

Our relationships do not have the time to wait while we postpone allowing God to get his hands on our controlling, critical spirits. The children in our lives do not have the time to wait while we spiritualize away our fear and perfectionism. Our health does not have the time to wait while we live in denial of those issues that have the potential of shortening our lives. The lost certainly do not have the time to wait while we keep waiting until we are more "together" before we do something sacrificial for the sake of their souls.

It is time.

We all come from different places. Some of our pasts have been more immersed in crises. Some of our presents are more immersed in pain. And some of us have had choices stolen from us through abuse, disease, death, and divorce. But there is one choice that no one can steal from us, and that is our choice to follow God.

Day after day, choice after choice, every choice is a seed, every seed bears fruit.

May God strengthen us to plant well!

For Discussion and Reflective Journaling

Choose for yourselves this day whom you will serve.

Joshua 24:15

One. "Every choice plants a seed." Identify any choices you are currently making through "passive postponement."

Two. Picture your spiritual life as a garden. What adjectives would you use to describe its current condition?

newly planted	bug infested
recovering from pesticides	ready for something new
nurtured	covered in manure
forgotten	embarrassing
weedy	dry
fruitful	poorly guarded
in need of attention	postcard material

Three. People attend to the garden of their spirit for different reasons. Some want to avoid the embarrassment of others knowing they have weeds. Some want to be sure to not disqualify themselves from any blessings. Others feel compelled to pursue personal perfection. But these motivations produce only cosmetic change. For change to be deep and lasting, our motivation must be God-centered. Consider the following prayer as you recommit to choosing well, especially in difficult areas of your life:

Father God, you are trustworthy.
I invite you to be the gardener of my soul.
Walk with me through the garden of my life
and grant me the courage to see what is growing there.
Reveal truth, not for appearance's sake,
but so that I may love you more purely.
Transform me, not for perfection's sake,
but so that I may reflect you more accurately to a needy world.
Help me day by day, moment by moment to choose life.

This devotional and the discussion questions are excerpted from the DVD and participant workbook for Alicia Britt Chole's *Choices: To Be or Not to Be a Woman of God* Bible study curriculum (Rogersville, MO: onewholeworld, inc., 2003).

Beyond Prioritization, Part One

Early in my faith walk, a Bible study on time management introduced me to the tool of prioritization. I found the concept both helpful and stressful. When I was barely nineteen years old, a sheet of paper was placed before me and I was instructed to list the five most important things in my life.

> *Number one? God! That was easy*, I penned blissfully, beginning to write the next number on the page.
>
> *Number two?*
>
> (pause)
>
> *Numero dos?*
>
> *Umm*, I wondered, as my thoughts spun about like tires on mud. *Family? Ministry? School/Work? Church? The lost? My heart?*

Each option had a scriptural precedent as far as I could tell. When everyone had put down his or her pens, it occurred to me that perhaps I was overthinking the issue (shocker), so I decided to do it later as homework.

Then the leader handed us another "tool"—a weeklong time inventory. Shudder if you can. On this handy-dandy sheet, we were to log in EVERY ten minutes of our lives for two weeks. At the end, we were to tally up the categories of our actual use of time and share our reflections.

Some in the group took the task less than seriously when informed that no one would ever see their tallies. It made no difference to me: I was on a mission. So for the next fourteen days, I painstakingly kept track of every minute and when finished with the tally, I fell to the floor in tearful repentance:

> "Oh God! I still don't know what number two is, but it's obvious that number one is not you. If my first priority were you, I would spend more time with you than anything else. The results are clear: I serve the god of slumber!!"

True story. Yes, I was a somewhat dramatic teen, suffering (no doubt) from PMS. Nonetheless, early on in life I had a head-on collision with the limitations of prioritization.

Thankfully, God was poised to offer me another, more livable tool.

For Discussion and Reflective Journaling

But seek first his kingdom and his righteousness, and all these things will be given to you as well.
Matthew 6:33

One. Have you ever struggled trying to determine what should be first, second, third, fourth, and so on, in your life? If so, in what areas is this struggle the greatest?

Two. What does *"seek first his kingdom and his righteousness"* mean to you?

Three. Write down your top five priorities. (I will spare you the time sheet—though it is an excellent exercise.) But instead of listing them numerically, attempt to draw them as five concentric circles. Start in the middle with the priority that influences all others *the most* and working outward with the final ring reserved for the priority that influences the others *the least.*

Beyond Prioritization, Part Two

In purpose, prioritization enables us to evaluate opportunities and responsibilities in light of our values and primary objectives. However, in practice, prioritization alone can lead us to focus on something, cross it off our list, and mentally go on with our day. For example, we can have our devotions in the morning, then—grateful that God has been honored "first" in our day—we can easily cross God off our list mentally and go on with the next task.

Long ago God asked me a question while I was worshiping him on the piano: "*Alicia, who is the center of your life?*" Without hesitation I answered, "You are!" His response stunned me. "*No, child, you are,*" he said. "*You've made me first, but you are still your center.*"

I had prioritized God, but I had not centralized God. What a difference!

When something is centered, it can never be completed or crossed off. It can only expand.

When something is centered, it cannot be contained by "first," "second," or "third." It is core.

When something is centered, it cannot be reduced to a task. It becomes a motivating force.

God wanted to be centralized in my life. Beyond first, he desired to be my center of gravity regardless of what I happened to be doing or what role I happened to be fulfilling.

He is my center of gravity as a daughter, wife, and mother. He is my core as a speaker and writer. He is my motivation as I serve and share.

Is God first? Yes, but much more than first, he is at the center of all that I am and all that I do.

And that, for this rather analytical artist, was liberating indeed.

For Discussion and Reflective Journaling

Then I saw a Lamb, looking as if it had been slain, standing in the center of the throne, encircled by the four living creatures and the elders.

Revelation 5:6

For the Lamb at the center of the throne will be their shepherd; he will lead them to springs of living water.

Revelation 7:17

One. These pictures from Revelation are breathtaking. Spend a few minutes trying to imagine the scenes these verses paint for us.

Two. I find the images in the book of Revelation to be intensely beautiful and overwhelmingly full of mystery. One truth is clear to me, though: if Jesus is at the center in heaven, he should be at the center of my life on earth. In your own words, what is the difference between prioritizing God and centralizing God?

Three. Over the next few days, remind yourself often that in addition to being first, Jesus is also at the very center of your life. Journal any differences in attitude you note as you consciously acknowledge the centrality of God throughout your days.

Dear God . . .

I Think I'm Doing All the Talking

Taking Turns

In Genesis 18:23 Abraham asked God: *"Will you sweep away the righteous with the wicked?"*

From David in Psalm 13:1 we hear: *"How long, O Lord? Will you forget me forever? How long will you hide your face from me?"*

Jeremiah, in Jeremiah 12:1, cries: *"You are always righteous, O Lord, when I bring a case before you. Yet I would speak with you about your justice: Why does the way of the wicked prosper? Why do all the faithless live at ease?"*

Abraham, David, Jeremiah.

Patriarchs, kings, and prophets *all* asked questions of God.

The difference often between these forefathers and us and is not that we have questions and they did not. The difference is that, when they had questions, they took turns.

They asked . . . and then remembered God's Word.

They asked . . . and then listened for God's voice.

They asked . . . and then they waited.

Yet all too often,

We ask . . . and then remember our troubles.

We ask . . . and then listen to other voices.

We ask . . . and then we leave.

If we question without giving God a turn—if we question without waiting, listening, and remembering—we are in danger of cultivating resentment or arrogance.

But if we ask questions and then honor God by waiting, listening, and remembering, we cultivate dependence and humility.

And God's very Presence can answer our questioning hearts at depths words cannot penetrate.

For Discussion and Reflective Journaling

In the morning, O LORD, you hear my voice;
in the morning I lay my requests before you
and wait in expectation.

Psalm 5:3

One. On a scale of 1 (Are you kidding?!) to 10 (I feel complete freedom), how easy is it for you to ask the kind of questions Abraham, David, and Jeremiah directed to God?

Two. Personally, God most often speaks to me through the Bible, through the lives of my children, and through nature. When I am still, he inclines my thoughts in his direction and places principles and questions in my mind. How does God "speak" to you?

Three. Though few would describe God as "chatty," spiritually it is still beneficial to "take turns" when we speak with him; to pause, to wait, to listen. Today, as you conclude your devotional time, follow the example of David in Psalm 5:3: lay your requests before God and then "wait in expectation."

A Gift . . . or a Habit?

"Keona," I hear Jonathan moan from upstairs, "please, can you just stop talking for FIVE minutes? I have a headache."

"Mommy says that talking is my gift," Keona retorts.

"It's a habit," Jonathan attempts.

"Gift!"

"Habit!"

"GIFT!"

"HABIT!"

Then in stereo: "MOM!!"

It is true: our precious daughter loves to talk. In fact, I think I can safely say that I have never in my entire life met anyone who loves to talk as much as Keona. Thankfully, when Keona talks, she actually says something. Her words are always meaningful and often entertaining. Baby girl has a captivating personality.

Recently a few language experts came to our home to evaluate our youngest for a speech delay. "There may be more going on," the speech pathologist offered, "but my guess is that Louie doesn't talk because he doesn't *need* to talk."

"Excuse me?" I asked.

"Louie isn't talking because perhaps other siblings . . . (at this point she paused to give a less than subtle nod toward big sister) . . . are doing all the talking for him."

"Ah," we said, smiling at our gifted talker.

Extended grace to our daughter is easy. First, she is only five. Second, she is absolutely delightful. Third, she reminds me of myself. No, I was never a constant talker in people's presence. I was a constant talker in God's presence.

Early on, my "quiet times" were anything but quiet. Though I may not have spoken aloud, my devotional life was a crowded one-way street of me talking to God; reading, praying, thinking, asking—busily directing my thoughts toward him.

Then a wise someone placed two books in my hands: Dick Eastman's *The Hour That Changed the World* and Richard Foster's *Celebration of Discipline*. Whoever you are, I—and (no doubt) God—thank you profusely.

These books introduced me to the discipline of silence and the art of prayerful waiting. A whole new world opened before me.

Decades later I have the joy of introducing these concepts to my captivating daughter during our "mommy-and-me mentoring moments."

Yes, I know she is only five. That is okay. I think the head start will serve her well.

For Discussion and Reflective Journaling

She [Martha] had a sister called Mary, who sat at the Lord's feet listening to what he said.

Luke 10:39

One. In *Creative Prayer*, Bridgid Herman states, "The most formidable enemy of the spiritual life and the last to be conquered is self-deception; and if there is a better cure for self-deception than silence it has yet to be discovered."[3] Prayerfully think about the connection between noisy living and self-deception. How can silence unveil deception?

Two. Consider Psalm 130:5–6: *"I wait for the LORD, my soul waits, and in his word I put my hope. My soul waits for the Lord more than watchmen wait for the morning, more than watchmen wait for the morning.* " Earlier generations often spoke of "waiting" on the Lord. Is the "waiting" spoken of by the psalmist familiar or unfamiliar to you?

Three. Spend a few moments evaluating the "quiet" in your quiet time. Are you comfortable or uncomfortable with silence? What role does listening/silence have in your prayer life?

Four. Try an experiment: Carve out three to five minutes each day to simply rest in God's presence. Just *be,* without reading, speaking, asking, singing, or working. Honor God with a few minutes of silence and stillness and then journal about your discoveries.

Wiggle Worms

The doctors eyed my parents with suspicion. "How did she cut her chin open *this* time?" "In the bathtub," Mom and Dad replied with sincerity. "She hates taking baths. She screams and squirms. We do our best to keep her safe, but she slipped out of our arms once again . . ."

Strange but true.

I was a wiggler and a wailer in the bathtub as a toddler. My poor parents endured the neighbors' raised eyebrows, the doctor's questions, and my pitiful puppy eyes in pursuit of their goal that I would slough off the daily grime and emerge sparkling before bedtime.

Not that I had any special affinity for dirt. In fact I loved being clean. I simply did not like *the process*.

How much easier it would have been for all involved if I had simply yielded and allowed my parents to get their cleansing hands on me. How much more quickly and painlessly we could have all arrived at their desired goal and my desired outcome if I had simply gotten *still*.

True then physically. True now spiritually.

We all long to slough off the old and embrace the new, to become centered in God, at peace through his Word, at rest in his love . . . but we struggle with letting God get his cleansing hands on us. We are spiritual wiggle worms.

Two decades after my squirmy toddler days, gentle Jesus began to open my eyes to the strength of stillness.

He invited me to stop squirming, resist wiggling, and start relishing the ancient discipline of waiting on him. Peace is weather-proofed through stillness. Hope becomes muscular as we meditate on God's truth. Whether or not we tangibly sense his presence, our spirit is refreshed and renewed as we focus our thoughts on God.

The change we all long for is not found in going faster. Lasting change is found in getting still.

For Discussion and Reflective Journaling

Be still before the LORD and wait patiently for him.
Psalm 37:7

One. How natural is it for you to "be still"? To "wait patiently"?

Two. When was the last time you saw an advertisement emphasizing "It goes slower!" as a selling point? When I was younger, a selling point for the quality of ketchup was how slowly it moved. The accompanying jingle sang a catchy, "an-ti-ci-pa-a-tion . . . is making you wait." Now even ketchup comes in speedy squeezable bottles. Our culture screams that to get farther you must go faster. Yet God's Word speaks of going slower to get deeper.

Write down at least five adjectives that you would like to accurately describe your relationship with God five years from today.

Three. "The change we all long for is not found in going faster. Lasting change is found in getting still." Summarize this principle in your own words and then offer them to God in the form of a prayer.

A Tin Chapel

"There's Jesus walking with Mommy," my son whispered to Daddy while they watched from a distance as Sister Emmanuel and I walked together up the gravel path. Wrapped in blue, her face radiated relationship with the living God. "Not Jesus, but Jesus' friend," my husband explained to our precious little boy.

Jonathan requested the Sister's hand and together they escorted me to a tin cottage nestled in the trees. Confident that Mommy was safe, Daddy and son gave me kisses and left me in the cottage-turned-chapel for two days of prayer.

Unpacking in silence, I recalled my first prayer retreat. Years ago I considered these times of focused prayer a luxury. Now my husband and I are convinced that prayer retreats are a true necessity for our family.

A wobbly desk, a fraying patch of carpet, bare walls—the simplicity of the place stood in stark contrast against the neon and clutter of our world.

Slowly, hour by hour, the solitude increased my awareness that I am never alone.

Reading, listening . . . the God who is always near soothed my anxious heart with his Word. His truth was like warm oil on my dry spirit.

Writing, walking . . . relaxing in God's presence, resting in God's acceptance. Simultaneously I knew my sinfulness and God's love. Such gracious love warrants gratitude-filled pauses in my days and life.

Waiting . . . on God. Waiting because God is worthy of our waiting—whether or not he speaks. The treasures of waiting are many, but the greatest of these is God himself.

My hope is that through these sacred spaces of prayer-filled pauses, more of Jesus will be visible through me. My hope is that, even without a godly saint by my side, my children will be able to say, "There's Jesus. He walks with my mommy."

For Discussion and Reflective Journaling

Come with me by yourselves to a quiet place and get some rest.

Mark 6:31

One. Henri Nouwen suggested that we dedicate one hour a day, one afternoon a week, one day a month, and one week a year to prayer retreats with Jesus. "What a dream!" we sigh. But all dreams begin with a breath. All walks begin with a step. Take a few moments to ask Jesus how you could carve out more alone time in your life. Write down your thoughts and begin to make plans toward your retreats—be they for fifteen minutes or entire days.

Two. What attitudes currently capture your approach to, and time with, God? Duty or discovery? Habit or hope? God is infinitely creative. He is speaking, he is waiting, and he is longing for us to discover him anew every day.

Three. Conclude your discovery time with God in silence. Unlike other forms of meditation, Christian meditation is not an emptying of our minds but a focusing of our thoughts exclusively on God. Begin thinking of adjectives that describe God (pure, trustworthy, near) and then wait before him, letting those adjectives simmer in your soul. Silence refreshes our spirits as sleep refreshes our bodies.

Dear God . . .

Why Do I Feel So

Unproductive?

Building Muscle

"Alicia, I—" she began and then paused searching for words. "I know that I am doing the most important thing on earth in focusing on my baby. I feel awful even saying this. Why do I feel so unproductive?"

Bright, gifted, and extremely capable, this dear woman is currently using her framed master's degree as a paperweight.

Whether or not we have diaper rash cream in every room of the house, most of us experience chapters of life in which we are not utilizing our professional skills and training. We have postponed schooling, hopped off the career ladder, declined advancement . . . and chosen a less-driven pace to focus on something we deem "better."

When obedience leads us into such seasons, what does productivity look like? When our résumés are not growing, what is?

In a word: character.

No, I am not remotely suggesting that character somehow stagnates in the marketplace. But when obedience leads us to decrease visibly—in what the world sees and applauds—that decrease creates a unique opportunity to increase spiritually in what God sees and applauds.

The challenge is, however, that productivity looks different in such seasons. Instead of being praised for completed projects, we are given countless occasions to make peace with the incomplete. Instead of being promoted for being "first," we are given numerous opportunities to find joy in being last.

This different type of growth reminds me of the counsel I received from a fitness trainer. (Please do not be too impressed. I have not stepped inside a gym since my third child was born.) He explained that at first I would feel as though I were really making progress, because the initial fat burn would be easily visible. "Then," he cautioned, "you'll come to me and ask what's wrong because you're not seeing as much change. Don't be fooled and don't be discouraged. That's when the real work is occurring. It means you're starting to build muscle."

Building muscle (and building character) is a different type of productivity.

It is less visible.

And more powerful.

In fact character growth is the "real work" of life.

For Discussion and Reflective Journaling

We also rejoice in our sufferings, because we know that suffering produces perseverance; perseverance, character; and character, hope.

Romans 5:3–4

One. In your own words, summarize this mother's struggle regarding productivity. Is this challenge in any way familiar to you?

Two. In this passage in Romans, the Greek word translated as *sufferings* (*thlipsis*) is more often translated as *trouble(s)*. Looking back over the last year, are you able to identify some "troubles" that produced character in you?

Three. Consider again the wisdom in the fitness trainer's words. Then conclude by thanking God for how he is building muscle (character) in you currently through your circumstances. This invisible work of character growth is a form of productivity that will outlast this lifetime.

In Winter

A century ago a few fragile seeds fell on rocky soil. Through drought and flood, they clung tightly to earth, stubbornly stretching toward the heavens. Today silver maple, post oak, and black walnut trees surround our home like tall, loyal sentinels. Their intricate, mingled root systems support the ground below. Their long, angular boughs weave a canopy above. Before I was, they were. My elders by many decades, their presence is steadying.

In the heat, I rest under the covering of their rich foliage. Bursting with shades of green, the leaves dance in the breeze. Winter's reduction is coming, but that does not halt the dance. Trees celebrate the moment, temporary though it is. In the spring, their new growth sings of hope. Their lush greenery offers peace in the summer. In the fall, their colorful collages inspire creativity. And in their emptiness, trees grace the winter with silent elegance.

Though my skin prefers their role in summer, somehow my soul prefers their lessons in winter. Then, when growth pauses, the trees have often become my teachers.

What the plenty of summer hides, the nakedness of winter reveals: infrastructure. Fullness often distracts from foundations. But in the stillness of winter, the trees' true strength is unveiled. Stripped of decoration, the tree trunks become prominent.

As a child I always colored tree trunks brown, but to my adult eyes they appear to be more of a warm gray. Starting with their thick bases, I begin studying each tree. Buckling strips of bark clothe mile after mile of weathered branches. Leafless, the trees feature their intricate support systems. Detail is visible, as is dead wood. Lifeless limbs concealed by summer's boasting are now exposed.

My eyes glide from one rough, uneven bough to another and then to the terminal, delicate twigs. A tree's posture is all open, like arms ready for an embrace. So very vulnerable, yet so very strong. I find the display quieting and full of grace.

> In winter, are the trees bare? Yes.
> In winter, are the trees barren? No.

Life still is.

Life does not sleep—though in winter she retracts all advertisement. And when she does so, she is conserving and preparing for the future.

And so it is with us. Seasonally, we too are stripped of visible fruit. Our giftings are hidden; our abilities are underestimated. When previous successes fade and current efforts falter, we can easily mistake the fruitlessness for failure.

But such is the rhythm of spiritual life: new growth, fruitfulness, transition, rest . . . new growth, fruitfulness, transition, rest. Abundance may make us feel more productive, but perhaps emptiness has greater power to strengthen our souls.

In spiritual winters, our fullness is thinned so that—undistracted by our giftings—we can focus on our character. In the absence of anything to measure, we are left with nothing to stare at except for our foundation.

Risking inspection, we begin to examine the motivations that support our deeds, the attitudes that influence our words, the dead wood otherwise hidden beneath our busyness. Then a life-changing transition occurs as we move from resistance through repentance to the place of rest. With gratitude, we simply abide. Like a tree planted by living water, we focus on our primary responsibility: remaining in him.

In winter are we bare? Yes.
In winter are we barren? No.

True life still is.

The Father's work in us does not sleep—though in spiritual winters he retracts all advertisement. And when he does so, he is purifying our faith, strengthening our character, conserving our energy, and preparing us for the future.

The sleepy days of winter hide us so that seductive days of summer will not ruin us.

For Discussion and Reflective Journaling

He is like a tree planted by streams of water, which yields its fruit in season.
Psalm 1:3

One. Winter, spring, summer, fall: Which is your favorite season? Why?

Two. When you think of your God-given abilities and potential, which season most accurately depicts your life today: The seeming barrenness of winter? The new growth of spring? The fullness of summer? The transitions of fall?

Three. What adjectives would you use to describe how you feel about this season?

Four. Offer these feelings to God, asking him to strengthen you to be like the tree spoken of in Psalm 1—a tree planted by streams of water that bears its fruit in season.

This devotional is reprinted with publisher's permission from Alicia Britt Chole's book *Anonymous: Jesus' Hidden Years and Yours* (Nashville: Nelson, 2005), 1–3. The discussion questions are excerpted from the reflective study guide of Alicia Britt Chole's *Anonymous: Jesus' Hidden Years and Yours Bible study curriculum* (Rogersville, MO: onewholeworld, inc., 2008).

Surfer Girl (Sort Of)

This is reality, not humility: I was a lousy surfer. Nonetheless, every weekend—weather permitting—I would strap my six-foot-two-inch, twin fin, Danny (or was it Tony?) Holt New Image surfboard onto the truck and drive an hour to the beach.

Apart from hurricane season, South Padre is not necessarily known for its surf, which makes my lack of skill even more lacking. Pulling up to the shore, I would drink in the sea breeze, wax up my board, head into the water . . . and most of the time it would end there with me sitting or floating on the board as a wannabe surfer girl.

However, from time to time I would actually try to catch a wave and—if feeling especially adventurous—even attempt going past one set of waves to catch a bigger set on the other side.

That pilgrimage from smaller to larger waves requires a great deal of upper body strength. You have to stay balanced on the board and use your arms as paddles to slice through the first break and reach the calm before the next set of waves hits you.

The pros (well, most people) do it effortlessly. But not me. I swallowed gallons of salt water, found myself under the board as much as on top of it, and had a knack for navigating straight into—as opposed to through—crashing sets of waves. However, once in a while I would emerge (exhausted) on *the other side.*

The other side offered a few moments of rest. Another set of waves was coming for sure. Without question they would be bigger, be stronger, and require more skill to ride. But for a minute there was a calm to take a deep breath, recover from what was, and prepare for what was to come.

That experience returns to me now, one or two or twenty-something years removed from South Padre Island. Now, when teenagers (the polite ones) call me "ma'am" and with a gasp shout, "GET OUT! *You* were a surfer?"

Yes, now my surfer days return to me as I find myself "in between" breaks in the ocean of real life.

The last set of waves was a challenge to navigate, extremely fruitful, and extremely full. Now I am "in between" what was and what will be, in the pause before a transition in life and ministry. In this pause, I hear Father God whispering, "*Rest, my child. Do not strain to see the next set of waves. Do not stress over whether you will be able to ride them well. Do not wonder if they will be more this or less that. Simply rest.*"

Logically, the next set of waves you and I will face in our lives will be stronger, be bigger, and require more skill to navigate. Now, however, guessing what *will be* is not our primary concern. The calling of those "in between" is to faithful waiting and intentional resting.

Divine pauses are rich with potential. Whether they last a few weeks or a few years, these seeming lulls are gifts from God.

For Discussion and Reflective Journaling

Teach us to number our days aright,
that we may gain a heart of wisdom.
Psalm 90:12

One. Where would you place yourself in this illustration?

- Trying to navigate a new set of waves
- In the lull between the last set and the next set of waves

- Staring at the next set of waves, wondering if you should turn around and head back to the car
- Under the board, swallowing sand
- Out to lunch

Two. Sometimes lulls can last so long that they feel like oceans in and of themselves. In such seasons, it is tempting to expend energy wondering what lies ahead. Think back on your most recent challenging season. Did you enter it rested? In what specific ways do you think being rested might benefit your next challenging season?

Three. If you currently find yourself "in between," consider adding something from the following list to your plans for rest and renewal:

- Take time to pamper your soul.
  - Take a prayer retreat.
  - Begin a new devotional book or Bible study.
  - Take daily walks alone with Jesus.
  - Start a gratitude journal.
  - Listen to worship music.
- Soberly evaluate and enhance your state of health.
  - Take a class on healthy eating.
  - Consult a fitness trainer.
  - Begin an exercise plan.
  - Get a massage.
- Nurture friendships.
  - Reconnect with a dear old friend.
  - Ask someone new to have coffee.
  - Write a thank-you letter to a teacher or mentor.

- Expand your mind.
  - Take a pottery class.
  - Sign up for music lessons.
  - Visit your library.
  - Join a book club.
- Attend to loose ends at a peaceful pace.
  - Organize photos.
  - Finish a project.
  - Write thank-you notes.
- And . . .

Hidden Years

What news! God is pleased with my hidden years. He does not view anonymous seasons as boring and unfortunate preludes to rush through quickly so I can move on to some other season that is more productive and exciting.

And though I am sure that God, like any parent, finds joy in every season of our lives, it will not surprise me if in the end we learn that he enjoyed our hidden years the most. They seem less cluttered with the glittery stuff that distracts us from His face.

My children[4] are in their hidden years. They are dancing blissfully in almost complete anonymity. With the exception of a few other privileged souls, my husband and I are their primary audience. How we treasure the show!

Our son's belly laugh—if bottled—could further the cause of world peace. His compassion regularly causes my eyes to leak. Jonathan sends every single penny he has to "the poor children . . . because they do not have milk or bananas or computers." And it is still very hard for him to understand why all the planet's orphans cannot come live with us in our house. He's concerned for the world, but without apology he adores his mommy! Once when I was in bed looking pretty puny, he came into my room holding a glass. Taking a drink, he then offered the glass to me and said, "Here, Mommy, drink after me so you can catch my healthy."

Our daughter is liquid sunshine. She's brilliant, beautiful, and dramatic! In a moment of complete silence at a solemn ceremony that was being projected on the big screen, Keona shouted, "Look! I AM ON T.V.!!!!" She feels deeply, tells you about it loudly, and gets over it quickly. And by nature, she's a nurturer. Following my unexpected surgery, two-year-old Keona would daily ask, "Mommy, are you better yet?" and then proceed to comb my hair with her toothbrush and smash gobs of Vaseline between my toes. I'll never forget the first time after that surgery when I was able to walk down the stairs on my own. While I sat at the bottom catching my breath, Keona came up and asked if she could hold me. Then with her beautiful arms wrapped around me, she whispered, "Mommy, I am so proud of you."

You didn't know about all that, did you? Nope. And that is okay. These moments have taken place during hidden years that only a few hearts have been graced to observe.

As far as the world is concerned, my children are living in anonymity. Jonathan is yet to realize his unusual blend of exceptional abilities. Keona is still unaware of her striking gift of influence. They're currently unable to take a stand against injustice, research cures for cancer, or even tie their own shoes. They are hidden. And they are the delight of our hearts.

My husband and I treasure beyond words our private viewing of Jonathan's and Keona's hidden years. Our front row seats in their lives are priceless. We are their greatest fans and for the moment, they are not looking for any others. We are enough. How nice it is to be enough!

I wonder if in my own life, God feels like I believe he is enough.

Soon we'll have competition. Soon others will be impressed by Jonathan's genius and dazzled by Keona's inner and outer beauty. Soon my children will have to navigate through praise and applause, criticism and rejection. Soon the room will be filled with flattering admirers and unwelcome detractors.

But my hope is that our presence and, more importantly, the presence of Jesus that we keep drawing their attention to, will steady them. We were there before the crowds came and he will be there after my husband and I and the crowds have to leave.

In hidden years, Father God is our only consistent audience. Others come and others go, but only he always sees. God alone realizes our full potential and comprehends the longings in our souls. When no one else is interested in (let alone impressed by) our capabilities and dreams, God is still wholeheartedly, with fatherly pride shouting his love over us.

Anonymous seasons afford us the opportunity to establish God as our souls' true point of reference *if* we resist underestimating how he treasures our hiddenness and take the time to decide whose attention and acceptance really matters in our lives.

For Discussion and Reflective Journaling

Your life is now hidden with Christ in God.
Colossians 3:3

One. Have you ever felt hidden? Which, if any, of the following experiences are familiar to you?

- Moving to a new place where no one knows your name
- Entering a different environment where others underestimate your experience
- Returning to school to sit as a learner once again
- Shifting from professional recognition to the relative anonymity of focusing on family
- Resigning a title and realizing that the phone has stopped ringing
- Walking through crisis and having to place your personal dreams on hold

Two. According to the devotional, how does God view your hidden years?

Three. Picture God in the front row of your life beaming and shouting louder than the proudest soccer mom. Is this image easy or hard for you to accept?

Four. Many grow up being affirmed more for visible accomplishments than for invisible character. Take a few moments to reflect on your relationship with God. Do you think that he is withholding "I'm proud of you, my child" until you attain a certain position or achieve a specific goal? Why or why not?

Five. Finally, think of the children in your life. Soberly ask yourself if you are treasuring their hidden years.

This devotional is reprinted with publisher's permission from Alicia Britt Chole's book *Anonymous*, 45–47. The discussion questions are excerpted from the reflective study guide for *Anonymous*.

Dear God . . .

The Grass Is Really Looking Greener Elsewhere

The Cows Just Came Home

All wrapped up in black and white polka-dots, a classic collection of our neighbor's cows look longingly at our lawn.

The Polka-dots regularly make the hundred-acre pilgrimage to our fence line. Passing rich pasture, they wander to the edge of their domain then crane their necks through the barbed wire fence to nibble at our exotic, "gourmet" grass—which is identical to the grass they stand and do other things on.

I watch them from my writing room on the second floor and smile. The Polka-dots possess many virtues, no doubt, but they lack perspective.

They seem oblivious to the riches of their own home. How short-sighted!

They wound themselves by pressing past boundaries their master has set for them. How foolish!

They mourn what they cannot have instead of delighting in what has been given to them. How ungrateful!

How much . . . like me.

The cows just came home.

I watch them from my writing room and go to my knees in prayer.

For Discussion and Reflective Journaling

LORD, you have assigned me my portion and
    my cup;
    you have made my lot secure.

**The boundary lines have fallen for me in
pleasant places;
surely I have a delightful inheritance.**
Psalm 16:5–6

One. Our culture injects us with strong doses of dissatisfaction. Countless millions of hours and dollars have been invested in discovering what makes us, the consumer, crave. How hard it is to resist absorbing the continuous stream of suggestions that we need something more, something different, something better! And if we need it, then surely it exists "out there" beyond where we currently live. In light of this overt, ever-present agenda of consumerism in our culture, reflect on the truth contained in the above verses. Weigh each word carefully.

Two. Webster's defines *assign* as "(1) To set aside for a particular purpose: designate. (2) To select for a duty or office: appoint. (3) To give out as a task: allot." In this passage, David the psalmist recognizes the directing and sustaining hand of God in the bigger picture of his life. This perspective fills him with rejoicing, not regret; with security, not restlessness.

Our good Father God assigns each of us a portion from his hand. Spend a few moments intentionally evaluating your life from the perspective of what you have been given, not what you have yet to get; from the perspective of what currently is good, not by what good you are still waiting for.

Three. Conclude your reflections with thanksgiving. Thank God for his involvement in your life. Thank him for the portion he has assigned, for the boundary lines he has established. Ask him to help you see today through his eternal eyes.

This devotional is reprinted from Alicia Britt Chole's *Pure Joy* (Nashville: Nelson, 2003).

Attainable

In politics, academia, the marketplace, and even the church, many express frustration over the presence of *glass ceilings*—invisible yet real barriers to opportunity or advancement. These ceilings are built by the opinions and choices of those in power. When one is shattered, all rejoice.

Rejoice: there is no glass ceiling between you and God. A splintered cross shattered it long ago. Jesus endured the cruelty of crucifixion to pay for our sins with his death. Through Jesus' sacrifice, Father God holds a high opinion of us, his forgiven ones.

> The ceiling separating us from God has been
>   shattered.
> Rejoice: Intimacy with him is attainable.

No circumstance can doom us to a stale, stagnated spirituality. Neither the death of loved ones nor the departure of near ones can destine us for demise. Neither diseases nor disasters can decree that failure is inevitable.

> The ceiling separating us from God has been
>   shattered.
> Rejoice: Intimacy with him is attainable.

No season can doom us to just limp along with an out-of-date, out-of-breath faith. Neither parenthood nor retirement can destine us to "just hold on until . . ." Neither extended studies nor tough transitions can decree that anemic faith is our fate.

> The ceiling separating us from God has been
> shattered.
> Rejoice: Intimacy with him is attainable.

God's greatest desire is for us to know him both now and forevermore. Coupled with the reality that God does not waste time, I am absolutely convinced that every moment of every season is an opportunity for spiritual growth.

Sometimes that growth is visible; often it is invisible. Sometimes that growth is immediate; often it takes time. Sometimes that growth is celebrated; often it is underestimated.

But even when invisible, time-intensive, and underestimated, growth still *is*.

Spiritual intimacy is not a luxury reserved only for those able to devote themselves to a life of solitary prayer. Whatever the circumstance, whatever the season, today introduced a fresh opportunity to nurture relationship with God.

> The ceiling separating us from God has been
> shattered.
> Rejoice: Intimacy with him is attainable.

For Discussion and Reflective Journaling

But you are a chosen people, a royal priesthood, a holy nation, a people belonging to God, that you may declare the praises of him who called you out of darkness into his wonderful light.

1 Peter 2:9

One. In God's presence, ask yourself if you have ever felt that there was a glass ceiling to the intimacy you could experience with him. This sense of spiritual limitation can arise from remorse over past failures, stress over pressing matters, helplessness over others' choices, or even doubts about our ability or God's character.

Two. Often a sense of discontentment arises from a belief that we are "stuck," that something we long for is unattainable because of our current circumstances. While this may be true academically or even financially, this is never true spiritually. This season of life is as rich with possibilities for intimacy with God as any ever has been and any ever will be. Begin your time of reflection by turning to God in prayer and asking him to open your eyes to this season's spiritual potential.

Three. In Romans 8:39, Paul declares that nothing *"can separate us from the love of God."* Truly, because of Jesus' sacrifice, there are no barriers to intimacy with God. Conclude your time of reflection with thanksgiving to God for the potential of "now."

This Too

What activities in life are holy? Webster's defines *holy* as "exalted, divine, devoted entirely to deity or the work of deity."

What activities in life qualify as worship? Webster's defines *worship* as "reverence offered a divine being."

Is being a pastor more holy than being a parent?

Is singing more worshipful than serving?

I do not think so.

Our motivations can make the simplest task holy or the most impressive deed dead. Our attitudes can make the smallest act worship or the grandest offering bankrupt.

This is cause for celebration for the sincere in heart: every season of life is overflowing with potential to live a holy, worshipful existence.

When I was single, solitude was holy.

When newly married, two-now-one was worship.

When I became a mother, life together was both.

Even this morning, I was reminded of how pleased Father God is when we offer him our ordinary moments. Baby Louie is our family alarm clock. He wakes up, rain or shine, at 6:30 a.m. Eventually, all three children climb in bed with us.

Keona normally comes in first, carrying her pillow and wedging herself between Barry and me. She snuggles close, and I breathe in the refreshing scent of her peppermint hair cream. Then Jonathan emerges sleepily from his room, says "Morning!" and goes to the restroom. Crawling into our bed, he closes his eyes as I kiss his warm porcelain cheek and shake my head remembering how he used to fit in my hands.

The next ten to thirty minutes are filled with quiet cuddles and questions about life. When wiggly baby Louie joins us, we all become fences around the queen bed's perimeter to keep him from bouncing off.

Before entering parenthood, Barry and I would always get up and offer the first part of our day to God through songs, walks, extended readings, and quiet times. Today I gazed into the eyes of my loving kids, touched their soft faces, and smiled as I looked at the clock.

My Bible, journal, piano would still be waiting for me later in the day. But I knew that Father God was smiling over these morning moments as well. I could almost hear God whisper as I hugged and loved on his kids:

"Ah, this too is holy. This too is worship."

For Discussion and Reflective Journaling

And do not forget to do good and to share with others, for with such sacrifices God is pleased.
Hebrews 13:16

One. "God is pleased." Three words to treasure! Look back over the last twenty-four hours and remember the small things you did that served, shared, or did good for others.

Two. Whether or not the people we served noticed, God saw each act of service and was very pleased. It is important, however, that we learn to be satisfied with God's "well done." When God's pleasure is not enough for us, we can slip into martyrdom and serve resentfully or even begin to emotionally punish others for not noticing our "sacrifices." Take a few moments in prayer asking God to ensure that your service remains clean and free from resentment.

Three. We began this reflection by looking back. We will conclude by looking forward. Consider what awaits you in the next twenty-four hours. In prayer, offer your forthcoming opportunities *"to do good and to share with others"* to God.

I'll Show You

"Why?!!" the kids cried as Barry relayed the sad news that their overnight plans with the grandparents had to be cancelled.

Extreme disappointment (unfortunately) is somewhat invulnerable to logic. Barry knew that this was not the moment to explain how freezing rain is formed. Disappointment is rarely dissolved by charts and graphs.

"WHY?" they asked again with increased volume and tears in their voices.

Extreme disappointment (unfortunately) is somewhat lacking in patience. Barry knew this was not the moment to put the teakettle on the stove and invite the kids to evaluate their emotions while meditating on Claude Debussy's "Clair de Lune." Disappointment is rarely defused by discussion, culture, and a hot cup of tea.

Pausing, Barry looked lovingly into their eyes and simply said, "Let me show you why. Everyone put your shoes on."

This was unexpected. Action? Something physical? Their disappointment temporarily distracted by a task, the kids quickly put their shoes on, and Dad opened the door.

Having an innate aversion to cold temperatures (as in, say, under 75° F), I went to watch from the upstairs window. Whines of frustration quickly gave way to squeals of delight as the kids slipped and slid over the driveway.

Barry gave them a few minutes to play and then said, "This is *why*. If you can't walk on the road, it's not wise to drive on the road."

They were convinced. He allowed them to *feel* the logic, instead of just *hear* the logic. He had the patience to *reveal* the answer when they did not have the patience to *hear* the answer.

And he was not done yet. Surprising even me, Barry then leaned over the car's window and in the forming ice carved out a tic-tac-toe grid. They took turns for one short game, and without even a whisper Daddy was saying, "And we can still have fun."

I never heard another whimper about the change of plans.

Wise dad? Yes, and a principle to remember next time we are disappointed.

Often we wonder why God does not simply *explain* things to us. "Surely our disappointment would dissolve if he would just tell us the *why* behind his actions and choices," we moan.

Instead, God often seems silent in our moments of greatest frustration. Even then, God is near. He is wisely withholding his words knowing that extreme disappointment is rarely tamed by logic or by lecture.

If we listen, we may hear him inviting us to put our shoes on, to go outside—to do something physical and seemingly unrelated. If we watch, we may find him holding our hand, while we slip about and see something unexpected.

Reminding ourselves of God's faithful, fatherly presence can take the edge off—and the sting out of—our disappointment long before anything logical fills in the empty blanks of our angst.

Truly, God is the wisest teacher of all.

For Discussion and Reflective Journaling

Good and upright is the LORD;
  therefore he instructs sinners in his ways.
He guides the humble in what is right
  and teaches them his way.
All the ways of the LORD are loving and
  faithful

for those who keep the demands of his
covenant.
Psalm 25:8–10

One. How do you respond—emotionally, physically, spiritually—
when you are deeply disappointed (for example, pout, sleep, think
the world is coming to an end, lash out, withdraw, etc.)?

Two. Drawing from your experience with children, what is the
wisest response when someone is irrationally frustrated? Has God
ever used this response with you?

Three. Sometimes disappointment's power is in its vagueness. Write
down specifically anything you are disappointed about.

Four. Then bring each disappointment before God in prayer.
Whether or not you perceive that God is involved in the disappointment, affirm in faith that he is indeed a wise teacher. Ask
him to help you grow in recognizing his fatherly presence in the
midst of disappointment.

Dear God . . .

Today My Faith

Feels Frail

In His Grip

Unplanned. Unwanted. Today the unexpected occurred.

Ever since she could remember, little Teresa loved holding her daddy's finger as they walked together. She held on tightly determined to never let him go. She knew if she stayed by his side, all would be well.

Walking to their waiting car, Teresa looked up to see a truck racing through the parking lot. There was no time—the truck was moving too fast. There was no choice—she would be hit. Without even thinking, she did what she thought she would never do. In fear, little Teresa let go of her daddy's finger.

But little Teresa's daddy was a good father. He expected the unplanned. He anticipated the unwanted. He had seen the truck before little Teresa had felt the first tremor of fear.

And all along, while Teresa held on to her daddy's finger, her daddy had wrapped his hand firmly around her wrist.

As the truck sped toward Teresa, her daddy tightened his grip. As Teresa in fear let go, her father lifted her up and carried her to safety. Then her daddy held Teresa in his arms while fear loosened its hold on her heart.

As I said, he was a good daddy.

We too hold tightly to our Father God's finger, determined to never let him go; confident that our commitment, our experience, and our intellect are the forces that alone bind us to our God.

Then the unexpected occurs. Unplanned, unwanted, in fear we feel our hold loosening as pain presses us, as the unknown casts shadows on our soul.

But all along, our faithful Father has firmly gripped us by his Spirit. He is the Author and Guardian of our faith.

In the time of trouble, he tightens his invisible yet eternal grip on us and carries us to safety. Then Father God offers to hold us in his arms while fear loosens its hold on our hearts.

Safe in his arms, we gratefully, with reaffirmed childlike faith, echo the confidence of David the psalmist:

> *You hem me in—behind and before;*
> *you have laid your hand upon me.*
> *Such knowledge is too wonderful for me,*
> *too lofty for me to attain. . . .*
> *If I rise on the wings of the dawn,*
> *if I settle on the far side of the sea,*
> *even there your hand will guide me,*
> *your right hand will hold me fast.*
> *Psalm 139:5–6, 9–10*

For Discussion and Reflective Journaling

You hem me in—behind and before.
Psalm 139:5

One. Wrapped securely around your intellectual, emotional, and experiential hold on faith are the presence and power of God himself. Perhaps even recently events have unnerved you and loosened your grip on faith. Meditate on the truth that, like the father in this devotional, God saw what was coming and began activating his power to keep you long before you felt the first tremor of fear.

Two. The parking lot story is an adaptation of an experience relayed to me by one of my first pastors. In other words, it is a true story. Like Teresa, we need to treasure the one who holds our hand. Picture God's strong hand gripping your wrist as you hold tightly to his finger.

Three. Conclude your time of reflection by reading Hebrews 12:2–3 and recommitting your unknown future to God's care:

> *Let us fix our eyes on Jesus, the author and perfecter of our faith, who for the joy set before him endured the cross, scorning its shame, and sat down at the right hand of the throne of God. Consider him who endured such opposition from sinful men, so that you will not grow weary and lose heart.*
>
> *Hebrews 12:2–3*

Undeleted Scenes

"I wouldn't have written the script of my life this way, Father God."

"What would you have changed, Child?"

"I would have deleted unnecessary pain."

"What kind of pain is that?"

"Senseless misunderstandings, incurable illnesses, and undeserved injustice. These produce nothing but tears in my heart and aches in my soul. I could have done without them, Father."

"I too could have done without sin's shadows and pain's piercings. But because of choices made long ago and choices remade every moment, I myself had a choice to make: turn my back on sin's shadows or personally embrace pain's piercings."

"What did you choose, Father?"

"I chose the path of what you call 'unnecessary' pain."

"Why? How?"

"Actually, you helped me. Before you were born, Child, I saw you and my love for you was greater than life. Through sweat and blood I measured my love for you, and its passion fixed my life

willingly to a cross. By embracing pain, I robbed sin of its power to crush you."

"Then the shadows will not destroy me! But there are still tears in my heart and aches in my soul."

"Yes, Child. In mine as well. But even there you can find a treasure if you allow the tears in your heart and the aches in your soul to grow dependence on me in your spirit."

For Discussion and Reflective Journaling

And we know that in all things God works for the good of those who love him, who have been called according to his purpose.

Romans 8:28

One. This tender dialogue between Father and Child reflects on soul-bruises. If we think of our lives as a movie, all of us have scenes we wish could have been deleted or edited. These are the bruising memories that cause us to wince, to ache, to question, to move faster.

When you remember these scenes (intentionally or unintentionally), where is God in the picture? Absent? Present? Do you picture him watching? Sleeping? Helping? Protecting? Distracted? Critiquing? Take a few moments to consider the truth that God was and is as near to you as a mother is to the child in her womb.

Two. In this story, Father speaks of how his love for his child fastened his life to the cross. Consider the truth that God's intense love for you strengthened him to endure pain so that you could know freedom: *"For God so loved the world that he gave his one and only Son, that whoever believes in him shall not perish but have eternal life"* (John 3:16).

Three. This devotional refers to dependence as a "treasure." In a culture that applauds independence, valuing dependence can be a challenge. Choosing to be dependant on God is not a vote for passivity or weakness. Choosing to be dependant on God is a vote for active reliance—by dependence we intentionally immerse ourselves in God's strength. In the coming days, remind yourself that treasures can be found even in the place of pain by those who resist self-protection and embrace God-dependence.

When Dreams Die

Buried any dreams lately?

We thought our dreams were God's dreams. We prayed, believed, made plans, and worked hard. But now it is over.

So here we sit, graveside, by our lifeless hopes. And as we sit, we begin to doubt: Did I miss something? Should I have prayed or done more? Or perhaps I never really heard God in the first place . . . If this was not God's will, then how can I trust myself to ever think I hear him?!

Jesus' first disciples knew exactly how we feel. They too had a dream that was cruelly crucified before their very eyes. They were certain that their dream was God's dream, but then their hoped-for Messiah was murdered. Not even a fool could hope now. The sealed tomb confirmed the truth: Jesus was dead.

Today we speed-read through the darkest days of the disciples' lives because we know that the joy of the resurrection is only a few verses away. But if we slow down, there is much to learn. What did they do after their dream died on the cross? How did they cope? Let us walk with the disciples as they mourned the death of the greatest dream they had ever known:

> But all those who knew him . . . stood at a distance, watching these things. . . . [Joseph] asked for Jesus' body. Then he took it down, wrapped it in linen cloth, and placed it in a tomb cut in the rock, one in which no one had yet been laid.
>
> Luke 23:49, 52–53

Speechless, Jesus' followers kept watch until the very end. They held on to flickering hope until its flame was extinguished. Then they gave themselves permission to bury their dream. Burial is a symbol of respect.

When dreams shatter, we too need to give ourselves time to gently collect the broken pieces and wrap them respectfully in tears. This is not about prematurely abandoning hope. This is about accepting reality. Denying Jesus' death would not return him to the disciples. It was healthy for them to permit a burial. Faith is not threatened by funerals.

> *The women who had come with Jesus from Galilee followed Joseph and saw the tomb and how his body was laid in it. Then they went home and prepared spices and perfumes. But they rested on the Sabbath in obedience to the commandment.*
>
> *Luke 23:55–56*

Jesus' followers lingered by his tomb; then they returned home to prepare spices and oils to preserve and honor him in his death.

Those who have lost loved ones may need to linger in that favorite old chair. The entrepreneur may need unhurried days (instead of one angry hour) to reminisce as she packs up an office after an unsuccessful business venture. In response to that rejection letter, the student may need to head for the mountains to refresh her faith. Or the one who suffered a miscarriage may need to give herself permission to mourn instead of rushing to put everything away.

Take the time. Prepare the spices. Preserve and honor the memories. Rest. The women rested after Jesus' death. Rest is essential—a need, not a luxury—if we are to remain healthy through the burial of dreams.

Two of them were going to a village called Emmaus. . . .
They were talking with each other about everything that
had happened.
Luke 24:13–14

Like the followers of Jesus, when dreams die, we need to enjoy good talks and take long walks with trusted friends. The disciples did not isolate themselves after Jesus' burial. They intentionally maintained their relationships. We too must resist isolation. Even in loss, we are stronger together than alone.

As they talked and discussed these things with each other,
Jesus himself came up and walked along with them; but
they were kept from recognizing him.
Luke 24:15–16

The disciples did not know it but as they walked with each other, Jesus walked with them. They could not comprehend it, but their dream though dead had not perished!

Most of us will not see the resurrection of our dreams within three days. In fact some of our dreams are sown for future generations to reap. Even then, obedience is never a waste; it is an investment in a future we cannot see. When we dream with God, even in burial our dreams are not lost, they are planted. God never forgets the "*kernel of wheat [that] falls to the ground and dies*" (John 12:24).

What grows from that painful planting is God's business. But sowing in faith is ours and our faithfulness is never sown in vain.

For Discussion and Reflective Journaling

But you, O God, do see trouble and grief;
you consider it to take it in hand.
The victim commits himself to you;
you are the helper of the fatherless.
Psalm 10:14

One. Have you buried any dreams lately? In God's presence, pause to identify each dream specifically.

Two. What stands out to you the most about the disciples' journey after the greatest dream they had ever known died on the cross?

Three. Fill in the following statement for your current situation: When standing graveside by buried dreams, I personally need to _____ _____ (for example, give myself time to linger, not isolate myself, rest, or something else).

Four. ". . . our faithfulness is never sown in vain." Think about individuals whose faithfulness produced fruit in your life. Make an extra effort to—through a card, phone call, or email—let someone know that you are proof that their faithfulness was not sown in vain.

This devotional is reprinted with permission from Alicia Britt Chole's *Sitting in God's Sunshine, Resting in His Love* (Nashville: Thomas Nelson, 2005), 150–54.

Words for the Worried

This is not about caring; this is about fretting.

This is not about reasonable attention; this is about rising anxiety.

Jesus counseled, *"Do not worry about your life, what you will eat or drink; or about your body, what you will wear"* (Matthew 6:25).

In our stress-saturated world, it is easy to justify worry. "It is not a lack of trust," we rationalize; "it is the presence of concern." But when "concern" begins to furrow our brow, tie knots in our stomach, incite us to nibble on our nails, interfere with our sleep, and cause us to forget that God is our Provider, we can call it what we want, but God calls it worry.

Worriers come in at least three levels of intensity. There are the Occasional Worriers who seem generally immune to anxiety except for one or two significant areas like finances or their children or that odd pain in the back of their left ankle.

Then there are the Chronic (or constant) Worriers. Though busy, these worriers rarely celebrate the fruit of their labor. *Cannot spare the time*, they think as they immediately reroute their worry from one resolved crisis to a new, worthy cause. In fact Chronic Worriers never have a moment when their worry is not needed. They have causes and concerns lined up for years in advance.

Finally there are the Communal Worriers who have more capacity for worry than their lives can soak up, so they also worry for others. They even worry that others do not worry enough, which makes them more than a little vulnerable to nagging, but "at least they care enough to be concerned!"

In Matthew 6, Jesus identifies three principles that can help us win our war with worry.

Principle One: Worry Wastes, Not Stops, Time

Who of you by worrying can add a single hour to his life?

Matthew 6:27

Time is one of our most precious resources, but worry spends it like a fool. Worry takes our time without adding anything to our lives; not an hour to our day, an inch to our height, or a penny to our pocket.

Suppose we all lived in a very dry region. Every day we are given two gallons of water. We can (1) drink the water, (2) use it for cooking, (3) water our small gardens and grow food, or (4) pour it on the sidewalk or street. Most of us would choose some combination of 1, 2, and 3. But worry is like choosing 4.

Each day we are given a finite amount of emotional energy. How will we spend it? Taking care of daily needs for living, wisely preparing for the future, or worrying about everything that could go wrong?

Principle Two: God Knows What We Need

Do not worry, saying, "What shall we eat?" or "What shall we drink?" or "What shall we wear?" For the pagans run after all these things, and your heavenly Father knows that you need them.

Matthew 6:31–32

If God feeds the birds of the air and clothes the lilies of the field, he will certainly provide food and clothing for us. In every moment God knows exactly what we truly need and what we truly want. He is a good Father who will not fail to take care of his children.

Principle Three: Seeking God Is the Wisest Investment on Earth

Seek first his kingdom and his righteousness, and all these things will be given to you as well.
Matthew 6:33

When we spend the best of our energy seeking God, we find ourselves sufficiently provided for in every area of our lives. We become less anxious about the temporal because focusing on knowing God keeps our perspective on the eternal.

Worry, on the other hand, is an unwise investment. It cannot sew clothes to dress us, cook a meal to feed us, or build a house to shelter us. All it does is burn up our limited supply of daily energy in the smoky fire of fear.

Whether we worry occasionally, chronically, or for the whole community, these principles from Jesus can strengthen us to invest our time wisely in following God instead of wasting our time foolishly in wearisome worry.

For Discussion and Reflective Journaling

Therefore do not worry about tomorrow, for tomorrow will worry about itself. Each day has enough trouble of its own.
Matthew 6:34

One. Which, if any, of these three types of worriers do you most resemble: occasional, chronic, or communal?

Two. What do you worry about the most?

Three. Reconsider the example that worry is like pouring life-giving water on the street. Personally, when I worry, I lose sleep and gain tension headaches. What do you lose or gain from worry?

Four. Return to your answer for number two. In prayer, commit each worrisome issue to God, affirming in faith that he is a good and wise Father.

This devotional is reprinted with permission from Alicia Britt Chole's *Sitting in God's Sunshine*, 46–49.

Thirsty?

Like a silent stampede of silver gray stallions, the storm clouds raced across the evening sky. Swiftly they carried the hope of rain . . . away. Waiting watchers sighed and, with a silent prayer, returned to the drought.

Brittle brown fields, failing crops, low lake levels, anxious hearts. All longed for life-giving water.

Drought in our land is painfully visible. But another form of drought actually leaves us far more vulnerable to disaster.

Have you felt the pain of drought in your soul?

When hope has been carried away to another place
When emotions are brittle and snap under pressure
When sleep is diminished by a gnawing fear
When no place and no thing can quench a thirst deep within

The Samaritan woman described in John chapter 4 was well acquainted with drought of the soul. Broken relationships, secrets, rejection, whispers—her last reserves of hope were depleted by disappointment years ago. Standing in the noon sun by a weathered well, her hands were wet but her heart was dry.

Suddenly, Jesus spoke to her, *"Will you give me a drink?"* (John 4:7). Startled, she bowed her head, glancing down to avoid his eyes. His words trespassed propriety twice: Jews (his people) did not associate with Samaritans (her people), and most respectable people did not associate with someone like her at all.

Yet he had asked, so she dared to speak, *"You are a Jew and I am a Samaritan woman. How can you ask me for a drink?"* (John 4:9).

The stranger answered, *"If you knew the gift of God and who it is that asks you for a drink, you would have asked him and he would have given you living water"* (John 4:10).

A gift? From God? Of living water? Nonsense, she thought, her hands tightening around the worn rope. As water flooded her bucket, she found herself swallowing repeatedly, suddenly aware of her own thirst.

Motioning with his hand toward the well, the stranger continued, *"Everyone who drinks this water will be thirsty again, but whoever drinks the water I give him will never thirst. Indeed, the water I give him will become in him a spring of water welling up to eternal life"* (John 4:13–14).

Lifting her head, she studied the stranger. His dress, like hers, was simple. Rough sandals covered calloused feet. There was nothing noteworthy about him, except for his eyes. He spoke of water and his eyes shone like the sea—warm, deep, full of ancient wisdom. *"Sir,"* she asked, *"give me this water so that I won't get thirsty and have to keep coming here to draw water"* (John 4:15).

Their conversation navigated uncomfortably through her past failures, present traditions, and future hopes. Listening, she began to wonder, *Who is this stranger? Surely this is no ordinary man. Probably a teacher, perhaps a prophet, or—or—could he be the Messiah?!*

"Then Jesus declared, 'I who speak to you am he'" (John 4:26).

With these words, the bucket slipped from her fingers, spilling fresh water on the dusty road. A small puddle formed at her feet. She stood speechless, staring into Jesus' eyes. Then, deep within, her spirit comprehended what her mind could not contain. Taking its first breath, faith thundered in her soul and began to release drop after drop, then sheet upon sheet, of pure, life-giving water.

Is your soul thirsty? Does your heart feel parched deep within?

Jesus' offer of living water still stands. With tears, he has traced every brittle crack in our dry hearts. In the scorching heat of shame, in the blistering desert of regret, God himself offers to rest over us like a welcome cloud. He longs to release within us his sweet, strong, living rain of truth.

Will that release transform the scenery, the circumstances, of our lives? Unknown.

Will that release transform our very souls? Guaranteed.

Drought in our land is out of our hands. But drought in our hearts must begin its retreat at the sound of three simple words, "Jesus, I believe."

For Discussion and Reflective Journaling

> Jesus answered, "Everyone who drinks this water will be thirsty again, but whoever drinks the water I give him will never thirst. Indeed, the water I give him will become in him a spring of water welling up to eternal life."
>
> *John 4:13–14*

One. Drought can be devastating. Take a moment to remember a time in which you knew drought physically or spiritually.

Two. Replay Jesus' interaction with the Samaritan woman in your mind. What emotions might she have felt at the moment she realized who Jesus really was? How do you think her realization and reaction made Jesus feel?

Three. A few chapters later Jesus said, *"If anyone is thirsty, let him come to me and drink. Whoever believes in me, as the Scripture has said, streams of living water will flow from within him"* (John 7:37–38). Are you thirsty today? If so, turn to Jesus in prayer. His offer of living water has yet to expire.

Dear God . . .

I'm Not Sure That I Can Keep Going

The Journey Back from Collapse

Elijah was absolutely exhausted.

He faced and defeated 450 false prophets. He climbed a mountain to earnestly intercede for drought-ending rain. He ran for twenty-five miles, faster than the king's chariot. And now, in what should have been a moment of victory, wicked Jezebel sent word that she was planning to kill him.

That was it. He was done. The combination of post-ministry exhaustion and fear of man was just too much. Elijah ran for his life *"and prayed that he might die. 'I have had enough, LORD,' he said. 'Take my life; I am no better than my ancestors'"* (1 Kings 19:4).

Though few of us have faced several hundred prophets of Baal, we do understand extreme weariness. The stresses of work and finances, the strains of relationships and conflicts, and the realities of spiritual opposition leave us feeling fatigued. Add a crisis to that normal load, and we can collapse altogether.

How did Elijah journey from collapse to a place where he had the strength to obey God again? Typically to answer that question, we turn to Elijah's encounter with God on Mount Horeb. But even before his incredible mountain experience, Elijah was regaining strength in small and seemingly insignificant ways in the desert. How?

1. Elijah prayed. After running from Jezebel, an isolated Elijah plopped down under a scruffy tree in the desert and prayed.

Yes, it was a pretty miserable prayer, but he was still talking to God and every little bit helps!

2. Elijah slept. No instant cures exist for fatigue. Our bodies cannot be plugged into an outlet and revived in an hour. There are no substitutes for time and rest.

3. Elijah was touched by an angel. When we are exhausted, God sends his messengers to us in many forms: the hug of a child, a call from a friend, the touch of a loved one. God's arms are long enough to reach us, even in the desert.

4. Elijah ate. Some of us wish we would lose our appetite! But for those of us who actually do, we must remember to eat. In his state of weariness, Elijah enjoyed angelic cuisine.

5. Then Elijah encountered God on the mountain. After a very long walk, Elijah arrived at Mount Horeb. God instructed him to *"Go out and stand on the mountain in the presence of the* LORD, *for the* LORD *is about to pass by"* (1 Kings 19:11).

There Elijah saw a shattering wind, an earthquake, and a fire, *"but the Lord was not in"* them. During these three powerful events Elijah heard NOTHING, which could have been a bit frustrating. So perhaps we should not be surprised when we hear nothing also. And perhaps we should be encouraged that in the midst of silence—even when it is the last thing we want to hear—something in the waiting still works to strengthen our souls.

God was in the gentle whisper. There God and Elijah exchanged the identical dialogue they had in the cave:

> *Then a voice said to him, "What are you doing here, Elijah?" He replied, "I have been very zealous for the* LORD *God Almighty. The Israelites have rejected your covenant, broken down your altars, and put your prophets to death with the sword. I am the only one left, and now they are trying to kill me too."*
>
> *1 Kings 19:13–14*

Creativity runs low when we are exhausted. So Elijah repeated his previous response: "I have done my best but nothing seems to make a difference. I am all alone and some people would be happier if I were gone."

Elijah's words have not changed much from his prayer under the tree in the desert, but his weariness has obviously subsided because when God gives Elijah directions, the prophet has sufficient strength to obey.

Certainly the concentration of God's presence on the mountain strengthened Elijah, but God's presence in the desert carried him there. In minute yet meaningful ways, God's presence was refreshing Elijah all along as he slept and ate, walked and prayed, was touched by angels, and waited for God to speak.

As we journey from collapse back to a point where we have strength to obey, let us be careful not to underestimate the desert. The mountain is amazing, but the desert is equally full of God's presence to refresh our lives.

For Discussion and Reflective Journaling

The LORD said, "Go out and stand on the mountain in the presence of the LORD, for the LORD is about to pass by."

1 Kings 19:11

One. What principle or picture stands out to you the most from this devotional?

Two. On the mountain Elijah saw evidence of God's power but heard and felt nothing until God gently whispered. Have you ever been in a service or at a conference where it seemed that everyone was experiencing God but you? What encouragement can you find for those times from the example of Elijah?

Three. Close your time with thanksgiving for the deserts in your life, asking God to open your spiritual eyes to see how he is strengthening you in small but significant ways.

This devotional is reprinted with permission from Alicia Britt Chole's *Sitting in God's Sunshine*, 29–32.

Overload, Part One

"If something doesn't change soon, I'm going to break down or burn out."

"Once I finish the things I have to do, I don't have energy left to do the things I want to do."

"My reserves are depleted. There's nothing left for me to draw on."

Do any of these statements sound or feel familiar? If so, please bookmark this page and go borrow or buy a copy of *Margin* by Dr. Richard Swenson.[5]

I rarely recommend books. But if you let it, this book will definitely change, probably lengthen, and unquestionably enrich your life. *Margin* contains principles that my husband and I ask every person we mentor to absorb.

The dishes were the last straw for me. Barry and I had been burning the candle at both ends for over a decade. As single ministers (he in Texas and I in the Far East), we stayed up late, ate irregularly, exercised infrequently, always said yes—and never thought about it because we were so very thrilled to simply partner with Jesus in the Great Commission. When we married, we continued this pace as we poured out our lives for the love of university students.

Then a transition occurred where we needed to spend one year in constant travel to gather a team of committed individuals and churches who would partner with us for the next season of ministry.

Many churches will be familiar with this model of missionary itineration. The rationale behind the practice is that it keeps the faces and focuses of the missionaries fresh in the minds of those who support them, and it provides the opportunity for young and old to hear a "call" to serve. In theory, it is truly beautiful. In practice, it is insane unless you happen to be graced with hyperactivity and outrageous extroversion.

I am not.

As the miles clicked on the odometer, something else was clicking within me—a countdown to burnout.

For Discussion and Reflective Journaling

Come to me, all you who are weary and burdened, and I will give you rest.

Matthew 11:28

One. Have you ever been close to burnout or breakdown? If so, describe the circumstances that contributed to your exhaustion.

Two. From either your own experience or the experiences of close friends, list some ways to safeguard against this degree of debilitating weariness.

Three. Prayerfully respond to Jesus' invitation in Matthew 11:28 (above).

Overload, Part Two

Within six months, I was a zombie. Living out of a suitcase, having intimate conversations with people who were absolute strangers less than an hour before, searching for hotels at midnight, and eating way too many meals at Denny's did *not* make for healthy living physically or emotionally for my wiring.

Genetically far sturdier, Barry was tired but not at the point of collapse. When he heard me crying in the kitchen, he came running in to find his wife gripping the counter and unable to speak through her tears. There were no signs of blood. No opened letter. No phone message. All he could do was hold me.

Finally, I was able to sputter out, "There's dir—dir—dirty di—di—dishes in the si—si—sink."

Yep—the dishes did me in. This was clearly a case of no margin.

Picture a straight horizontal line with three points: A at the beginning, B about three-quarters down, and C at the end. According to Doctor Swenson, on a normal day God intends us to live between point A and B. The space between point B and C (called margin) is a reserve that builds for crises, the unexpected, and the "extra mile."

But in our culture we live between A and C each day: we use up that reserve in normal living. So when a crisis does occur, we have nothing to draw from and are pushed into overload. When overload extends, it inevitably leads to burnout.

Just as I rarely recommend books, I rarely use precious print space to summarize principles that others have already skillfully written about. Dr. Swenson's book, however, is a lifesaver that will help you rediscover the rest—spiritually, physically, emotionally, and relationally—that God refers to throughout the Bible. Read . . . and get ready for change.

For Discussion and Reflective Journaling

Take my yoke upon you and learn from me, for I am gentle and humble in heart, and you will find rest for your souls. For my yoke is easy and my burden is light.

Matthew 11:29–30

One. Draw out the ABC illustration from the devotional. Do you have a reserve built up emotionally? Physically? Spiritually?

Two. If so, what has helped build that reserve? If not, what has been a drain on that reserve?

Three. Jesus states that we can find rest for our souls by (1) taking his yoke, and (2) learning from him. His life changed the world, yet in the Scriptures he never appears frazzled, fried, or frustrated. We never see Jesus worrying, hurrying, or scurrying. Certainly there were tiring times where he went the extra mile, but he seemed to have sufficient reserves for those days. Next time you read through the Gospels, consider how Jesus structured his day. In between the timeless teachings, look for patterns in his daily life that contributed to rest and a healthy reserve for crisis.

Four. If you are currently in overload or even burnout, please ask for the prayers of friends and make an appointment with your doctor. You desperately need friends' intercession and support. And it would be wise to seek a doctor's counsel. Exhaustion can quickly lead to clinical depression, and many will affirm that the road back to health from depression can be a painfully long trek.

Life's Storms

As the thunder sounded in the distance, my dad and I exchanged smiles. Hearing the summons, we both rose and took our places on the deck. Side by side we sat in silence relishing the first movements of nature's symphony.

The wind carried to us the sweet promise of rain. The lightning danced to a rhythm it alone could hear. The clouds rolled like an ocean over our heads.

While the storm proclaimed nature's untamed beauty, I sat in perfect peace tucked under Dad's arm, and tears of contentment collected in my young eyes.

From the beginning, Dad was determined that his only child would not inherit fear. "There is nothing to fear," he would say as he scooped his baby girl up and carried me out to our chair. Over the decades, I grew to savor storms—they were an invitation to rest with my daddy.

Dad's arms can no longer hold me—I am reminded of that reality every time I hear a distant thunder. But Another still sits near me when the winds beat against my life.

Life's storms are rather impolite. They neither consider our calendars nor consult our hearts. Without requesting permission, they simply come.

But each time they come, our Father God smiles and whispers, "There is nothing to fear."

As the earth shakes and our dreams crumble, God extends to us his strong arms. As the wind howls and our faith trembles, God offers to hide us in himself.

Life's storms issue to us an invitation to rest with Father God. Nestled securely in his eternal embrace, even the most furious storm cannot crush our fragile hearts.

For Discussion and Reflective Journaling

[Jesus] got up and rebuked the winds and the waves, and it was completely calm. The men were amazed and asked, "What kind of man is this? Even the winds and the waves obey him!"

Matthew 8:26–27

One. If life's storms are currently sweeping across the landscape of your heart, make a concerted effort today to sit alone with Father God for a few moments. Foregoing trust in your own strength, picture yourself nestled within God's strong arms and give yourself permission to be weak in his presence.

Two. In that power-filled place of dependence, meditate on this Scripture prayer based on Psalm 91:1–4, 14–15:

> I choose to dwell in your shelter, Most High God.
> I rest in your almighty shadow.
> You are my refuge and my fortress. You are my God
>   and I trust you.
> You will save me from the enemy's schemes and
>   attacks.
> You cover me with your feathers, under your wings I
>   find refuge.
> Your faithfulness is my shield; I will not be afraid.
> I love you, Lord. I believe you will rescue me and pro-
>   tect me.
> I call on you today and I know you will answer me.
> You are with me in this time of trouble. I wait for
>   your deliverance.

Life's Storms

Three. One of the healthiest choices we can make when overwhelmed with life's storms is to intentionally offer prayers for others who are also in crisis. Consider the tremendous needs of others today. Pray Psalm 91 over their lives asking God to be the dwelling place of the homeless, to provide rest for the weary, and to be a fortress for the abused.

A Mule Named Sam

The mule's name was Sam. (And no, this is not the beginning of a weak joke.)

My normally wise husband had the idea of taking two of our international students on a sleigh ride through the beautiful snowy plains of North Dakota. We all hopped onto a homemade sleigh pulled by this unusually large mule. (Did I mention that the mule was big?)

After a few frozen miles, we stopped at a friend's house to warm up with a cup of hot chocolate. (Anyone who offers you hot chocolate in December in North Dakota is a friend.)

While the others were still saying good-bye, I stepped onto the sleigh and Mr. Mule turned around and looked at me. Being slightly analytical, I was processing whether or not Mr. Mule was trying to communicate with me when Sam took off! I flew up in the air and landed flat on the sleigh. As Mr. Mule began to bolt, I slid completely off the sleigh.

My back landed in a pile of fresh snow.

My head (and, obviously, my waist-length hair) also landed in something fresh—a fragrant pile of mule-poo. (Did I mention that Sam was a BIG mule?!)

I really do not remember much about the rest of that day anymore. I cannot recall how excited we were in the beginning to get on the sleigh. I could not tell you one pitiful piece of stunning scenery we saw during the ride. Because all that really matters in the end is how things end, and that ride ended in a pile of overgrown donkey dung.

Well, life is like a sleigh ride.

Because what really matters in the end is *not* how excited we were in the beginning or how dazzling we were in our prime. What will really matter in that moment called "end" is, simply, how we ended.

If this moment were the moment called "end," would you and I have ended well? Or would Jesus find us—in our thoughts or in secret places—lying in a fresh mess?

God is looking for good endings. And if you are still reading this, there is still time to end well!

For Discussion and Reflective Journaling

**To him who overcomes and does my will to the end,
I will give authority over the nations.**
Revelation 2:26

One. If today were the day called "end" for you, are there any areas you would want to clean up before presenting them to Jesus?

Two. All of us sin in many ways. But it is critically important that we not allow that shared reality to cause us to take sin less seriously. If you are currently aware of anything for which you need to ask God's forgiveness, pause now and take the time to come to God in repentance.

Three. Write down any "piles" that you frequently seem to stumble into; any situations, places, or areas in which you are especially vulnerable to sin. This week ask a trusted friend or mentor to partner with you in prayer for support and accountability.

Dear God . . .

I'm Withdrawing
and I Don't Know
Why

Truths That Set Me Free

Ours is a fun and fabulous story . . . meeting at a retreat . . . a destiny-shaping game of ping-pong . . . courtship across an ocean . . . a proposal in Australia . . . and then I hit a WALL.

Many friends and family members had already purchased their plane tickets when we had to inform them that the wedding was postponed "indefinitely."

It was me, not Barry. I was frozen with fear—though it took me several months to identify that root.

The dominoes started falling when I received news that a respected minister friend had an affair. In the weeks that followed, I watched helplessly as the ensuing chaos shattered his family, his ministry, and the wounded young woman he had seduced. I was speechless. The sobering news hung over me like a dense cloud that blocked the sun and—unbeknownst to me—fear started collecting in the shadows.

Barry noticed the distance. "Are you okay?" he would ask. "I don't know," I would reply. Something was shifting within. I had less patience with Barry. I was more critical. I started to question our love and to withdraw my emotional investment in response to a nameless substance.

The wedding was off. A time of fasting had begun.

Returning home from a year of campus ministry in Australia, I spent countless hours on my face in prayer, eventually realizing that the nameless substance was called *fear*. I was afraid that it might happen to us: "What if unfaithfulness touches our love?! We are no stronger than this man was. We too have clay feet," I cried out desperately before God.

Fear of failure had gripped me. Through those weeks of weeping in my church's sanctuary, God showed me that my personal response to fear was to become more controlling. I analyzed and critiqued Barry, subconsciously looking for a reason to excuse myself from loving and committing my life to him.

In those dark months Barry tenaciously held on to God while God tenaciously held on to me and seized the opportunity to sow three truths in my soul.

(to be continued)

For Discussion and Reflective Journaling

Let love and faithfulness never leave you;
bind them around your neck,
write them on the tablet of your heart.
Proverbs 3:3

One. My precious husband refers to the month that I froze up and called off the wedding as "dark December." Dark it was! I was extremely confused and only vaguely aware of how deeply the news of the minister's failure had affected me. On a scale of 1 (not remotely) to 10 (a daily struggle), how vulnerable do you feel to fear?

Two. Most often, what are your fears focused on (for example, finances, children, health)?

Three. When gripped by the fear of failure, I became more critical and controlling. How do you respond when afraid? What does fear produce in you?

Four. Occasionally, some say that if Jesus were physically beside them, they would not be afraid. If you have the time, read Mark 4:35–41, a story in which those within arm's reach of Jesus were still paralyzed by fear. What do you think truly helps someone develop an immunity to the power of fear?

Truths That Set Me Free

Truth One: Regardless of how she cloaks herself, fear will always be our foe.

Fear is a master of disguise. She introduces herself as Caution, and we sit at her feet. She introduces herself as Wisdom, and we listen to her, unguarded. She introduces herself as Just Being Prepared, and we invite her to help us plan for the future.

As the clouds began to dissipate in my mind, it became painfully clear that I had formed an alliance with fear. I thought with fear and planned with fear. I asked fear to counsel me so I could avoid problems and stay one step ahead of pain. I requested fear to advise me so that disappointments would not catch me by surprise and disasters would not find me unprepared.

The minister's failure had thrown oil on the fire of fear, but I had been tending that flame for years. In practice, I called fear my friend and invested an enormous amount of energy considering "what could go wrong" scenarios and preparing myself for them . . . just in case.

At this point some readers are asking, "What on earth is Alicia talking about?" and others are saying, "Dear God, this is where I *live*!" If you are in the former group, feel free to skip the next two chapters and continue with the book. If you are in the latter group, though, please read on.

Consider the following verses:

The fear of the LORD is pure, enduring forever.
Psalm 19:9

Blessed is the man who fears the LORD,
who finds great delight in his commands. . . .
He will have no fear of bad news;
his heart is steadfast, trusting in the LORD.
His heart is secure, he will have no fear.
Psalm 112:1, 7–8

God did not give us a spirit of timidity [fearful apprehension], but a spirit of power, of love and of self-discipline.
2 Timothy 1:7

Without question, my fear was *not* pure. I *did* fear bad news. My heart was *not* at peace and my mind *was* apprehensive. I lived "on alert," ever vigilant to protect myself from—and prepare myself for—potential pain.

In short, I had to repent and ask God's forgiveness for aligning myself with fear. This was a key turning point for me spiritually. I still remember walking into the empty church nursery, kneeling on the worn carpet, and repenting sincerely—what freedom!

After that day, did I ever struggle with fear again? Yes, indeed. Marriage, ministry, and especially motherhood have all provided numerous opportunities for me to reaffirm the choice I made in the winter of 1990. But recognizing fear's disguises revoked fear's power in my life. Declaring fear a foe placed me safely on God's side in this battle. Through his Word and by his grace, every day I grow stronger in the fight.

For Discussion and Reflective Journaling

Preserve sound judgment and discernment,
do not let them out of your sight;

they will be life for you,
an ornament to grace your neck.
Then you will go on your way in safety,
and your foot will not stumble;
when you lie down, you will not be afraid;
when you lie down, your sleep will be
sweet.
Have no fear of sudden disaster
or of the ruin that overtakes the wicked,
for the LORD will be your confidence
and will keep your foot from being snared.
Proverbs 3:21–26

One. Have you ever "thought with fear" or "asked fear to counsel" you in an attempt to stay one step ahead of pain, problems, or crises?

Two. If the message of this devotional resonates with you, please carve out several minutes to respond in prayer. Read the Scriptures aloud and declare that fear is a foe. Ask God to forgive you for aligning yourself with fear and receive the cleansing Jesus provided for you on the cross.

Three. Personally, whenever I am tempted to feed fear, I have to actively engage my mind in something spiritually beneficial. Below I offer a list of personal strategies to fight fear. Feel free to add to, delete from, and edit this list into whatever will help you *"preserve sound judgment and discernment"* next time fear comes calling.

- pray for the needy
- focus on a Scripture I am trying to memorize
- pray Scripture
- open the Bible and read (aloud if possible)
- use my imagination to picture a relevant story from the Bible, like Jesus calming the storm or the angel being sent to shut the lions' mouths for Daniel

Truths That Set Me Free

Truth Two: It is inconsistent with God's character for him to be pleased by something that draws me away from him.

As I rose forgiven from that church nursery floor, God's sweet freedom was tangible. I wanted to immediately find a phone and call Barry with the news. Surely we could move forward now. Father God, no doubt, was smiling. Fear of failure was the loudest—but not the only—hindrance in my heart.

As a single woman, my views on marriage were mixed. On the one hand, I longed to share life with someone who loved God wholeheartedly. On the other hand, I feared that marriage would dilute the intimacy with God that I enjoyed. Yes, God's blessing on marriage was clear throughout the Scriptures, but equally clear was the fact that sometimes he called his servants to remain single.

So commenced another week of prayer and fasting: "Will marrying Barry draw me closer to you?" I asked. The question contained three critical components: marriage itself, marriage to Barry specifically, and marriage at that time of my life. The combination made my twenty-five-year-old brain hurt.

After a few days the real question became obvious: "God, how can I trust you to guide me?"

That is when I felt God pressing his words into my heart: *"Alicia, it pleases me for you to marry Barry."*

"Yes, thanks," I said, "but will it draw me closer to you?"

"It pleases me for you to marry Barry," he repeated.

Meditating on his words, the truth finally dawned on me: it is inconsistent with God's character for him to be pleased by something that draws me away from him.

A brief glance at the life of Mary, the mother of Jesus, makes it obvious that being led by God's pleasure neither grants us immunity to pain nor voids others' free wills. But regardless of what the future did or did not hold, as I searched through the Scriptures and sat alone in silence, a deep, enduring, anchoring confidence grew in my soul that my God was pleased with this specific choice.

God's character makes God's pleasure a trustworthy guide.

For Discussion and Reflective Journaling

"For I know the plans I have for you," declares the LORD, "plans to prosper you and not to harm you, plans to give you hope and a future. Then you will call upon me and come and pray to me, and I will listen to you. You will seek me and find me when you seek me with all your heart."

Jeremiah 29:11–13

One. "How can I know God's will?" is probably one of the most frequently asked questions by each generation. Write down some areas in which you are currently seeking to know God's will.

Two. The first source to consult when we are seeking to determine God's will is the Bible. Are there any stories or principles from Scripture that might be relevant to the decisions you are facing? For example, the Bible obviously did not contain a prophecy that said, "In 1990 Alicia should marry Barry." But the Scriptures were full of principles identifying the qualities a godly leader should possess (relevant when screening a potential spouse) and advice for those considering marriage.

Three. God has also graciously given us brains. If the Scriptures have not settled the issue, engage your brain matter further by, for example, listing the pros and cons and listening to the advice of those in authority in your life. (Note: Asking a trusted pastor or leader for his or her thoughts is quite a different matter than taking a poll from all your Facebook "friends.") Name those whom you would trust to give godly advice if you were facing a major decision.

Four. Having consulted God's Word, engaged your brain, and considered the advice of trusted leaders, you can take all this wisdom into a time of prayer and possibly fasting. Perhaps it is my personality, but my prayer times are not filled with fireworks. Over days, in the extended times of focusing on God, the anchor of his will begins to form in me and, eventually, I know what would please him. To be honest, if after all these steps, the way is still not clear, I normally assume that it is simply not time for me to make a decision yet.

Close your time today in prayer by affirming the truths contained in Jeremiah 29:11–13. Thank God that his plans for you are good and recommit to seeking him with all your heart.

Truths That Set Me Free

Truth Three: For each life, there is a path called obedience. It always leads to greater intimacy with God, and it always requires greater discipline to realize that greater intimacy.

With God's assurance in my heart, I finally phoned Barry, asked his forgiveness for how my fear-inspired criticisms had wounded him, and shared what God had shown me. Over the next several months, our relationship healed and we began to make plans for the wedding. Friends graciously agreed to book tickets again, and on June 23, 1990, my parents escorted me down the aisle toward the love of my life.

Saying our vows that day, I spoke mine with a deep confidence that this marriage pleased God—it was on his path of obedience for me. Consequently, I was certain that my union with Barry would draw me closer to God.

What I did not realize, though, was that this "drawing closer" would not be automatic.

What? I thought after the first few weeks. *Why didn't anyone prepare me for this? Shouldn't this be a topic of discussion in premarital counseling?*

I would start to worship . . . and someone would JOIN IN. I would be meditating on Scripture . . . and someone would ASK ME A QUESTION. I would be waiting on God in silence . . . and someone would START WHISTLING.

Imagine!

Poor Barry. This only child he had married had a *lot* of learning to do. Barry loved God with all of his heart. But the mere presence of someone else was cramping my devotional style. Gone were the days of just my Bible, my journal, and Jesus. Gone were the afternoons of complete solitude (Barry and I worked together) and the nights of glorious silence (he snored). Now someone was *with* me when I was *with* God.

To some, this probably sounds ridiculous. But many have shared with me how surprised they were that initially, marriage almost seemed to distract them from deepening their intimacy with God. For a few, the challenge was adjusting to drastically decreased solitude. For some, it was hard to carve out time to read the Word when they would rather be relaxing with their spouse. For others, they were so thrilled to finally have a human to talk with that they found themselves talking to God less.

And these challenges increase exponentially when—married or single—children are added to the recipe!

Greater intimacy requires greater discipline.

Over the years, greater discipline for me has included an expanded understanding of worship, increased communication with my family, flexibility with schedules, creativity in the use of time, and incorporating the practice of prayer retreats.

Where has the path of obedience led you? Whether into this ministry or that marketplace, into being single or being married, into being an auntie or being a mommy, that path *will* lead to greater intimacy with God.

(And it *will* require greater discipline to get there.)

For Discussion and Reflective Journaling

This is love for God: to obey his commands.
1 John 5:3

One. Describe any transitions or experiences that have disrupted the flow of your devotional life.

Two. "For each life, there is a path called obedience. It always leads to greater intimacy with God and it always requires greater discipline to realize that greater intimacy." Rephrase this principle in your own words.

Three. Perhaps with the help of friends, brainstorm creative ways in which you can become more disciplined in your pursuit of greater intimacy with God. Personally, because of our children's ages, my husband and I have to reassess our devotional lives every few months to keep them fresh and growing.

Dear God . . .

Why Do Those Who

Love You Suffer?

In the Midst of Suffering

Have you ever felt confused about God's faithfulness?

God is faithful . . . but his servants still know pain (consider Stephen who was stoned for speaking truth, Acts 7:59).

God is faithful . . . but his followers experience depression (consider the great prophet Elijah who prayed that he might die, 1 Kings 19:4).

God is faithful . . . but those who love him are familiar with loss (consider the prophetess Anna who was barren and widowed at a young age, Luke 2:36–37).

God is faithful . . . but his people endure injustice (consider Joseph who was sold into slavery by his jealous older brothers, Genesis 37:28).

Is God truly faithful . . . if his people suffer in this life?

In both the Old and New Testaments, the words used to describe God's faithfulness carry the meaning of truth, believability, and assurance. The writers of the Bible—who knew trouble and hardship in this world firsthand—unanimously confirm that God can be *trusted*, *relied on*, and *believed in*: He is a *faithful* God.

Moses proclaims, *"The LORD your God is God; he is the faithful God, keeping his covenant of love to a thousand generations of those who love him and keep his commands. . . . a faithful God who does no wrong, upright and just is he"* (Deuteronomy 7:9 and 32:4).

David asserts, *"All the ways of the LORD are loving and faithful for those who keep the demands of his covenant. . . . he is faithful in all he does"* (Psalms 25:10 and 33:4).

Jeremiah declares, *"Because of the* LORD'*s great love we are not consumed, for his compassions never fail. They are new every morning; great is your faithfulness"* (Lamentations 3:22–23).

Paul teaches, *"God, who has called you into fellowship with his Son Jesus Christ our Lord, is faithful"* (1 Corinthians 1:9).

Peter counsels, *"Those who suffer according to God's will should commit themselves to their faithful Creator and continue to do good"* (1 Peter 4:19).

And John affirms that Jesus *"is faithful and just"* (1 John 1:9).

These same writers understood rejection, betrayal, wars, hostile living conditions, the loss of children, and family strife. They were well acquainted with homelessness, false accusations, stonings, and emotional deserts. They knew sickness, deep discouragement, failure, bitter conflict, and persecution.

From their perspective, suffering did not invalidate God's faithfulness; suffering is where they experienced God's faithfulness.

We become confused because we falsely believe that the purpose of God's faithfulness is to prevent loss, shield us from all harm, and protect us from disappointment. But the writers of the Bible saw evidence of God's faithfulness not in their comfort level or circumstances but in God's constant companionship: God was with them—through the trials, fires, and aches of life.

God's faithfulness is not a passport out of trouble in this world. God's faithfulness is a promise of his presence in this world and in the world to come!

The faithfulness of God does not exist to keep us free from pain but to keep us focused on the path toward heaven. His faithfulness is not concentrated on the superficial or temporary. God has an eternal agenda: to faithfully guide our souls—through the suffering, loss, conflict, and pain of this world—into his everlasting arms.

So, as the writer of Hebrews encouraged:

> *Let us draw near to God with a sincere heart in full assurance of faith, having our hearts sprinkled to cleanse us*

*from a guilty conscience and having our bodies washed
with pure water. Let us hold unswervingly to the hope we
profess, for he who promised is faithful.*

Hebrews 10:22–23

For Discussion and Reflective Journaling

Here is a trustworthy saying: If we died with him,
we will also live with him; if we endure, we will also
reign with him. If we disown him, he will also disown
us; if we are faithless, he will remain faithful, for he
cannot disown himself.

2 Timothy 2:11–13

One. Throughout the Bible, those who spoke the most frequently
about God's faithfulness were extremely familiar with suffering.
How does our modern understanding of "faithfulness" contrast
with the biblical understanding of "faithfulness"?

Two. "Suffering did not invalidate God's faithfulness; suffering is
where they experienced God's faithfulness." Recall a time when
you knew God's faithfulness in the midst of suffering. What did
that experience grow in you?

Three. Today is so loud and tangible. Take a few moments to back
up from today and consider the reality that God is preparing you
for eternity. Journal your thoughts and discoveries.

My Son Cried Today

My son cried today.[6]

Walking into school, bigger children began to pour cruel words on him.

Though I intervened, their few words penetrated his mind like poison darts. My precious child fell to the floor and buried his head in the carpet. This mother's heart was ripped apart. I would do anything to shield him from such pain. Rejection is surely one of the most devastating wounds humanity inflicts on herself.

The ache only expands as I consider the rejection that may shadow my special son. His amazing mind sees the world in an unusual way. That gift makes him strong because it enables him to offer a unique contribution to this world for God. But that gift also makes him vulnerable because he is different.

Later during cuddle time, Jonathan whispered, "Mom, I'm *really* different. Like when I laugh, no one else does. I wish, I wish—"

"Yes, love?"

"I'm too shy to say it."

"Do you wish you weren't different?"

(silence)

In the light of the moon, I shared with Jonathan how different I always felt while growing up: the last kid picked for teams, the first kid others made fun of. I too have always seen the world in a different way. "Your difference is a gift," I assured him, "but it may take a long time for others to see and value that gift."

Staring into eyes that seemed too wise for his age, I told my son that Jesus was also very different and that people often hurt him with their words: "Since Jesus knows the pain of rejection, he can help us forgive others when they reject us."

Jonathan paused thoughtfully for a moment. Then, softly shaking his head, he said, "Okay, Mom," as he gave me a big bear hug.

Listening to his breathing as he fell asleep, I reflected on the pain of childhood peer rejection.

I contemplated the challenges my son was currently facing.

And I realized that I was crying.

For Discussion and Reflective Journaling

**The LORD is close to the brokenhearted
and saves those who are crushed in spirit.**
Psalm 34:18

One. Peer rejection was so pervasive and extended in my childhood that it actually contributed to a depression where I considered suicide in my early teens. Rejection is a powerful and persuasive force. How familiar were you with rejection as a child? As an adult?

Two. During another teachable moment, I shared with Jonathan that (1) people often say mean things because they have bruises in their hearts, and (2) letting mean words stick to you is like stepping on gum and then choosing not to remove it from your shoe: it can make you feel off balance and it causes dirt to stick to your soul. (No pun intended.)

Take an honest inventory of your heart. Is any "gum" sticking to your soul? In prayer, place into Jesus' pierced hands any wounding words and experiences that are haunting you.

Three. Close with a prayer of protection for the hearts, minds, and spirits of the children in your life.

Last Words

Like a gluttonous guest who arrived uninvited, cancer ate away at my friend's life. Nibble by nibble, bite by bite the disease shaved off the edges of her future.

Holding her hand, I was overwhelmed by the change. The tumor was growing rapidly. Andrea could no longer walk or move. I was not sure if I would ever hear her speak again.

Questions stirred restlessly in my soul: *What about her children? What about her husband? God, please do something!*

Few loved life like she did. Few loved people like she did. *Why, God? Where are the healings Jesus' voice brought to so many when he walked on this earth?*

Unoffended by my questioning, God gently brought his words to my memory:

> *Are not two sparrows sold for a penny? Yet not one of them will fall to the ground apart from the will of your Father. And even the very hairs of your head are all numbered. So don't be afraid.*
>
> Matthew 10:29–31

> *Precious in the sight of the* Lord *is the death of his saints.*
>
> Psalm 116:15

> *Who shall separate us from the love of Christ? Shall trouble or hardship or persecution or famine or nakedness or danger or sword? . . . I am convinced that neither death*

nor life, neither angels nor demons, neither the present nor
the future, not any powers, neither height nor depth, nor
anything else in all creation, will be able to separate us
from the love of God that is in Christ Jesus our Lord.
Romans 8:35, 38–39

Truth stabilized my answer-less heart. Suffering might steal my friend's strength, but no force in heaven or hell could steal the love of God from her life.

Then suddenly she opened her eyes and looked into mine. Smiling slightly, Andrea, with pain, formed the last words I ever heard her say. With her gentle southern accent she whispered, "L-luv . . . you."

Her peace passed understanding. God's love in and through her was stronger than life.

For Discussion and Reflective Journaling

I am always with you;
   you hold me by my right hand.
You guide me with your counsel,
   and afterward you will take me into glory.
Whom have I in heaven but you?
   And earth has nothing I desire besides you.
My flesh and my heart may fail,
   but God is the strength of my heart
   and my portion forever.
Psalm 73:23–26

One. Take a few moments to remember loved ones who have died. Thank God specifically for each one, remembering their unique contributions to your life.

Two. Write down before God any questions you have about their suffering or deaths.

Three. Read the Scriptures above again slowly, underlining (or jour-naling) each truth. For example, from Matthew 10:29–31 underline *"the very hairs of your head are all numbered."*

Four. Conclude by Scripture-praying these truths over the lives of those who are currently suffering. For example, "You, O God, have numbered the hairs on Becky's head. Strengthen her today not to be afraid."

A Special Gift

"Special needs," the doctor said, and all of the specialists nodded their heads.

"Special needs," written in whispers of ink over my child's life.

My son is more than precious to me. His smile warms my very soul.

He sees purely, feels deeply, loves sincerely.

His hug holds more healing than all the doctors in the world.

His "I love Mommy" carries more weight than all the applause of mankind.

My life is less than his. He has more to give, more to offer, more to share.

His "special needs" sing a duet with special strengths.

His love is not choked by the fear of rejection.

His opinions are not bribed by flattery or praise.

His giving is not oppressed by worry for tomorrow.

I too have "special needs." I need to be more like my special son.

"A special gift," the Creator said, and the heavenly host all nodded their heads.

For Discussion and Reflective Journaling

Those parts of the body that seem to be weaker are indispensable, and the parts that we think are less honorable we treat with special honor.

1 Corinthians 12:22–23

One. Each one of us has special needs, areas where we are painfully aware of our own weakness. Physical limitations, emotional scars, interpersonal wounds—nature and nurture both sow need in our world and in our souls. Still your heart for a few moments and ask God to be strong in your area of special need. For example: "Father, be strong in me as I grieve the loss of my loved one."

Two. Consider how King David sought to meet the needs of Jonathan's son Mephibosheth: *"Mephibosheth lived in Jerusalem, because he always ate at the king's table, and he was crippled in both feet"* (2 Samuel 9:13).

Three. This week seek to make a tangible difference in families touched by special needs. Find a practical way to serve them in the name of Jesus. Possibilities could include making a meal, cleaning house, mowing a lawn, bringing fresh flowers to a caregiver, or even joining with others to bless a family with mounting medical bills.

Four. How does God view those with special needs? Reflect on the following passage and then offer a prayer for those who *"seem to be weaker"* in the family:

> *The eye cannot say to the hand, "I don't need you!" And the head cannot say to the feet, "I don't need you!" On the contrary, those parts of the body that seem to be weaker are indispensable, and the parts that we think are less hon-*

orable we treat with special honor. And the parts that are unpresentable are treated with special modesty, while our presentable parts need no special treatment. But God has combined the members of the body and has given greater honor to the parts that lacked it, so that there should be no division in the body, but that its parts should have equal concern for each other.

1 Corinthians 12:21–25

This devotional is reprinted with permission from Alicia Britt Chole's *Pure Joy.*

Dear God...

Help Me See
as You See

The Call

The minister asked, "If you sense God's call into full-time ministry, would you please stand?"

The room exploded in applause as a few hundred teens stood with tears in their eyes. I held my breath and waited. And then my eyes filled with tears too, not for those who stood, but for the teens who were seated, the adults who were applauding, and the lost who are still waiting.

I had hoped to hear other calls, like, "Those of you who sense God's call to minister as educators, would you please stand?" (*applause*) "Those of you who feel God leading you into politics, the arts, the sciences, the home . . . would you please stand?" (*applause*)

But there were no other calls, no other applause. So what had we just communicated to those teens who remained seated? How must they have felt when, in integrity before Jesus, they knew the minister was not calling, and the church was not applauding, for people like them?

How easy it is for us as a church to applaud position. How easy it is to give more honor and attribute more value to those with certain titles and roles.

Unlike us, Jesus does not applaud position. He applauds obedience. His favor, delight, and power rest equally on all who follow him in obedience, regardless of whether obedience leads us to local neighborhoods or to Nepal, to public schools or to pulpits.

God definitely calls people to minister in traditional roles such as pastor, teacher, and evangelist. But I believe that he also calls people to minister as carpenters, professors, accountants, lawyers, secretaries, printers, musicians, linguists, navigators, cooks, coaches, nurses, artists, computer scientists, and parents.

Limiting "ministry" to the activity of professional clergy is like leaving the vast portion of a rich mine untouched. Jesus commissioned the *entire* church to be his witnesses *"to the ends of the earth"* (Acts 1:8). Fulfilling the Great Commission will require a world-size commitment from all of us. Together—and only together—can we reach our generation and the next.

For Discussion and Reflective Journaling

Therefore, if anyone is in Christ, he is a new creation; the old has gone, the new has come! All this is from God, who reconciled us to himself through Christ and gave us the ministry of reconciliation. . . . We are therefore Christ's ambassadors, as though God were making his appeal through us.

2 Corinthians 5:17–18, 20

One. How do you view the following activities? Are they ministry? Why or why not?

- pastoring a church
- parenting
- lecturing at a Bible school
- lecturing at a university
- caring for an abandoned child at an orphanage
- caring for a neglected child locally
- teaching missionary children in Brazil
- teaching public school children in Florida
- being an accountant for a church

- being an accountant for a company
- being a witness in your neighborhood
- being a witness as a waitress in a restaurant

Two. Consider your calling to partner with God in his great love for the world. List below any skills you have that *cannot* be used to serve God and others.

_____

_____

_____

_____

Three. Evidently all other skills *can* be used! Think about the abilities God has given you. Prayerfully conclude with a focus on ministry to your family. Wait on God for creative ways in which you can serve them today and remind yourself that in serving them in Jesus' name, you are faithfully participating in God's great mission.

This devotional is reprinted with permission from Alicia Britt Chole's Bible study *Until the Whole World Knows* (Rogersville, MO: onewholeworld, inc., 2000).

Near Not Far

At least three dozen birds are visible from my window this morning. Busily pecking at the frozen earth, they seem unaffected by the below-zero wind chill. Clearly, they are gathering food, but it appears haphazard, unscheduled, without choreography. Their disorderly dance brings a smile to my face.

How long were they there before I noticed them? I wonder.

I did not see them at first—I was too distracted by the distant rolling hills to look straight down. I was looking for inspiration from afar, not nearby.

In the time it took to type these sentences, every one of the three dozen has flown off to grace another space. I hope they will be noticed there.

Years ago I heard Dr. George O. Wood caution a group of leaders: "Focus your vision on what is small not big; what is near not far." His wise words took many by surprise. We are encouraged in our culture to wake up each morning and find clarity for living from the posted note on our mirror reminding us of our personal mission statement and five-year goals.

Please know that I have both (though I keep them in my journal instead of on my mirror). Such tools assist me in saying yes and no, in distinguishing between good and better. Personally, though, my inspiration for daily living comes from what is "small not big, near not far."

Even now I hear a disorderly dance and smile. My eldest is trying to groom the play chaos into something systematic in the family room. My middle is thrilled to have freedom to squeal and be LOUD without being asked to use her "inside voice." My youngest is gig-gling as he whips around the concrete floor on his scooter.

Life is abundant right here, right now.

Life is vibrant, tangible, and celebrated near me.

This is life on the ground—and it is glorious.

The birds have returned.
But this time I saw them come in one by one by one . . .

For Discussion and Reflective Journaling

Look at the birds of the air . . .
Matthew 6:26

One. Do you naturally look for inspiration from what is small or big? Near or far?

Two. If possible, take a moment to look outside and journal about what you see. How can that which is nearby inspire you today?

Three. Over the next few days, make a conscious effort to notice "life on the ground." Carry your journal with you to document children's quotes, loved ones' quirks, and nature's movements.

Four. Determine this week to celebrate the small and take pleasure in what God has placed within your arm's reach.

From Nay to Yea

Naysayers. Every season of life is "graced" with them.

When I broke an engagement in college because I did not have peace about getting married, the naysayers said, "Too bad. Good men are hard to come by."

(Today I am married to a very good man.)

When I graduated from college and went overseas to serve in the Far East, the naysayers said, "Too dangerous. You'll get sick."

(Today I am alive and grateful for good health.)

When I married, the naysayers said, "If you make it through the first year, you might be okay."

(The first year was glorious.)

Then they said, "Yeah, but watch out for the seventh year . . . and for the fifteenth year . . ."

(The seventh year was rich.)

(The fifteenth year was radiant.)

When I became a mother through the miracle of adoption, the naysayers said, "Congratulations, BUT—you might as well put ministry on hold for a few decades."

(These past twelve years have been among the most fruitful ministry years of my life.)

Now that our home is happily filled with children, they say, "Smile now—the terrible twos are coming for that one," or "You say it's a joy, but wait until they become teenagers."

(To date, I have treasured every month and year of my children's lives.)

And, to date, I still wonder why some feel the need to say "nay" in the face of happiness. Perhaps they sense a responsibility to warn others of what may come. Perhaps they project their fears on others' realities. Perhaps they assume that the challenges they encountered are a given for all.

Whatever the root, I find the fruit unpleasant.

Yes, I ached to be married after I broke the engagement. But God sowed spiritual intimacy in the soil of that loneliness.

Yes, I had my share of East-meets-West stomach viruses traveling overseas. But God sowed dependence in the soil of my weakness.

Yes, marriage has had its challenges. But God has sown character into the soil of mutual commitment.

Yes, as a mother of young children, I have less time to minister outside the home. But God has sown creativity into the soil of life-together.

And yes, on some days I give myself a time-out to think through a response to the most recent disobedience. But God has sown wisdom into the soil of child-raising.

Perhaps the difference between being a naysayer and being a yea-sayer is focus. The goal of life is not to avoid challenges, weaknesses, or crises. The goal of all living things is to grow (and multiply).

May God help us to . . .

grow with grace,

and multiply (grow others) with joy.

For Discussion and Reflective Journaling

For no matter how many promises God has made, they are "Yes" in Christ. And so through him the "Amen" is spoken by us to the glory of God.

2 Corinthians 1:20

153

One. By nurture and by nature, are you more inclined to be a nay-sayer or a yea-sayer, a vocal skeptic or an encouraging coach?

Two. If you have any nay-saying tendencies, ask God's help to replace doom-and-gloom predictions with faithful and fervent prayer.

Three. If your hope has been dulled by someone else's nay-saying ways, offer those discouraging words to God and ask him to replace them with his promises, which are "Yes" and "Amen."

Four. Consider once again these words from the devotional: "The goal of life is not to avoid challenges, weaknesses, or crises. The goal of all living things is to grow (and multiply)." Take these thoughts into a time of prayer as you ask Father God to help you see as he sees.

The Earth Is Hurting

My eldest son's perspective on life often causes me to pause.

He was ten when we were visited by a Noah-esque flood here in the Ozarks. Jonathan wanted to drink the rainwater, so he reached into the cupboard and pulled out a glass mug. As he started to head out the door, I asked him what would happen if the glass mug fell. I expected something like, "It could break" or "It might hurt me."

Instead, Jonathan—his voice filled with concern—said, "Oh! I should get a plastic mug because if the glass mug fell, it would hurt the earth and the earth is already hurting so, so very much!"

The earth is hurting?

I paused and thought:

God's earth respectfully absorbs the blood of martyrs.

It silently witnesses the abuse of children.

It graciously holds the tears of the broken.

Then I remembered the words of Romans 8:22–23:

> *We know that the whole creation has been groaning as in the pains of childbirth right up to the present time. Not only so, but we ourselves, who have the firstfruits of the Spirit, groan inwardly as we wait eagerly for our adoption as sons, the redemption of our bodies.*

The earth *is* hurting.

Jonathan already knew.

For Discussion and Reflective Journaling

> The creation waits in eager expectation for the sons of God to be revealed. For the creation was subjected to frustration, not by its own choice, but by the will of the one who subjected it, in hope that the creation itself will be liberated from its bondage to decay and brought into the glorious freedom of the children of God.
>
> *Romans 8:19–21*

One. Personally, I have been very challenged by Jonathan's natural concern for God's creation. He sees himself as a steward who will one day give an account for how he managed the resources entrusted to him. Sounds rather biblical and it affirms the basic sensibility that when you love someone, you respect (always) and take care of (as needed) their stuff. List the resources (the "stuff") that God has entrusted to you.

Two. How well do you feel you are doing at stewarding these resources? Write down any thoughts or ideas regarding how you can take care of God's gifts more respectfully.

Three. The greatest physical resource God has given you is life itself. How well are you taking care of yourself? In prayer, thank God for your life. Ask him to reveal any way in which you can be a better steward of the body and time he has given you.

Weasels of Faith

Weasels are brown, furry, slender mammals that feed on mice, moles, and small birds. They possess an interesting ability: weasels can suck the contents out of an egg without breaking its shell.

Empty, the gutted egg appears full.

Unbroken, the vacant egg seems whole.

Well fed, the weasel slips away with his deed unnoticed—for the moment.

Though instinctive and beneficial for the weasel, this ability paints a painfully accurate picture of something that is volitional and deadly for us—religious hypocrisy.

Webster's defines *hypocrisy* as "the act or practice of simulating or feigning to be what one is not; especially, the assuming of a false appearance of piety and virtue; insincerity."

Some of the harshest words in the entire New Testament were directed toward insincerity among those who claim to walk with God.

Jesus' description of hypocrites is recorded in Matthew 23:1–33:

- They proclaim truth but do not live what they preach (v. 3).
- They tithe but neglect to exercise justice, mercy, and faith (v. 23).
- They wash the outside of their dishes but fill the inside with greed and self-indulgence (v. 25).

- They are like sparkling tombs, beautiful without but full of death within (v. 27).

When we live hypocritically, we leave a trail like that of the weasel's eggs. Though gutted, we appear full. Though vacant, we seem whole—for the moment.

All of us stumble and sin in many ways. God graciously extends forgiveness to the repentant. But if we teach truth and knowingly live a lie, we are in grave danger.

Weasels may trick the eyes of other mammals. But who can escape the gaze of the all-knowing God? How grateful we can be for God's forgiveness and love!

For Discussion and Reflective Journaling

**Cleanse me with hyssop, and I will be clean;
wash me, and I will be whiter than snow.**
Psalm 51:7

One. Quiet your heart and then open your time of reflection by echoing David's prayer from Psalm 139:23–24: *"Search me, O God, and know my heart; test me and know my anxious thoughts. See if there is any offensive way in me, and lead me in the way everlasting."*

Two. With your journal in hand, spend five minutes waiting in God's presence. As he searches your heart, write down any areas of concern that he brings to your attention.

Three. Take these areas into a time of repentance. You may find it helpful to change your position to focus on repentance, perhaps by kneeling or bowing your head.

Four. During this prayerful time of repentance, be mindful of the following:

- any area God reveals but you do not want to write down
- any inclination to dilute the severity of sin or rationalize it away
- any effort to excuse actions by focusing on someone else's actions

Five. Conclude this time of cleansing with gratitude for our Forgiver, Jesus. Thank him for his blood that washes away all sin.

Dear God . . .

Please Refresh My Love for You

Anticipate

The darkness of night began its reluctant bow to a stronger force, the rising sun. Rich shades of yellow and orange overtook murky gray. Light chased down and then banished shadows as the sun's life-giving influence increased over the land.

Though not always visible, the sun always rises. Though not always felt, its warmth sustains life:

ever faithful,

ever giving,

always inviting,

always renewing.

Every morning, the sun rises over our lives.

And so too does our God. His mercy is new every morning. His love overtakes pain. His truth chases down and banishes deception.

Though not always visible, our God is always near. Though not always felt, his Word sustains all that is:

ever faithful,

ever giving,

always inviting,

always renewing.

Every morning, God rises over our lives.

While we sleep, he stands watch. When we awake, he smiles. Throughout our days he offers our busy hearts his life-giving influence.

Anticipate.

There is more of his goodness to explore. There is more of his healing to embrace. There is more of his warmth in which to rest.

Anticipate.

There is more of his truth to discover. There is more of his holiness to delight in. There is more in his heart that he longs to reveal.

Sit in his light. Bask in his warmth.

Rest in his love. Breathe in his Word.

God is rising over our lives.

For Discussion and Reflective Journaling

Because of the LORD's great love we are not consumed,
    for his compassions never fail.
They are new every morning;
    great is your faithfulness.
I say to myself, "The LORD is my portion;
    therefore I will wait for him."

The LORD is good to those whose hope is in him,
    to the one who seeks him;
it is good to wait quietly
    for the salvation of the LORD.
                                    Lamentations 3:22–26

One. List the attributes of God illustrated or identified in this devotional. Circle the ones that are most precious to you in this moment.

Two. Few things are more refreshing than a brilliant sunrise. Next time you have the opportunity to enjoy a sunrise, bring this list with you and thank God for each attribute as you relish one of God's most inspiring creations.

Three. The phrase "more of God" can be a bit confusing. If the infinite God is already with us, how can we have "more"? Yet it also captures a longing to see and experience God's truth, love, mercy, healing, and grace on a deeper, more pervasive level in our lives. Personally, there are several areas in which I literally ache to experience "more of God." If you also ache to experience more, bring these areas of longing before God in prayer. God also aches to pour out more of his "great love" and "compassion" on us, his children.

Pass a Tissue, Please

It happened.

When Jonathan was a baby, we spent time deliberating over the "What do we do about Santa Claus?" question. In the end, Jonathan's personality made the choice obvious. He was and is a fierce truth-seeking, black-and-white soul who desperately needs his parents' words to always be historically accurate and crystal clear. Jonathan is a master of justice who is mystified by inference.

So when four-year-old Keona asked about Santa Claus, the stage had already been set. "Yes, Santa Claus *is* real. He was a real person who lived long ago known as Saint Nicholas. . . . He is now in heaven but his real life inspired people through the centuries to celebrate the spirit of generosity and give sacrificially to help others . . ." Beautiful. Pass a tissue, please.

A few days later, though, Keona's teacher informed us that our normally wordy daughter reduced it all to just the facts. Though we had clearly explained the need to stay quiet when other kids talked about Santa Claus, Keona waited with her hand up at preschool while the teacher told a Santa Claus story.

"Yes, Keona?" Ms. Laura inquired. "You've been waiting so patiently so long. What would you like to say?"

"Santa's dead," Keona replied.

(Silence)

Thankfully, Ms. Laura recovered quickly, saved the day, and spared the class the brutal truth.

I would have lost sleep over it except that I was still recovering from that week's list of Jonathan's questions:

"Are *you* going through PUBERTY?!" (asked of every single person at the fourth through eighth grade mad-scientist gathering).

"Do you have any TEETH? You should go to the dentist!" (said to the elderly man being wheeled by his equally toothless daughter into the doctor's office).

"Do you have a BABY in your tummy?" (asked of anyone, male or female, with more than a twenty-four-inch waist).

Ah, child-speak is wonderfully unpredictable. Uncensored by long-term thinking, unedited by mistrust, the words of children lack pretense and fluff.

And Jesus says,

> *I tell you the truth, unless you change and become like little children, you will never enter the kingdom of heaven. Therefore, whoever humbles himself like this child is the greatest in the kingdom of heaven.*
>
> Matthew 18:3–4

No, I do not believe Jesus was giving us license to offend all our neighbors. I believe Jesus was challenging us to come to him without pretense.

Bringing our unedited selves to God can be humbling. We often prefer to clean up first. But in reality, that just delays true transformation.

When we come to God vulnerably, without censoring our feelings, we acknowledge and lean on a glorious truth: God knows us intimately, forgives us fully, and loves us completely.

For Discussion and Reflective Journaling

Here is a trustworthy saying that deserves full acceptance: Christ Jesus came into the world to save sin-

ners—of whom I am the worst. But for that very reason I was shown mercy so that in me, the worst of sinners, Christ Jesus might display his unlimited patience as an example for those who would believe on him and receive eternal life.

1 Timothy 1:15–16

One. All of us remember times when we would have gladly rewound or withdrawn our words had we been given the opportunity. A child's lack of pretense may be somewhat startling, but as adults, our lack of discretion can be disastrous. How wonderful that we can bring our unedited selves to God! Open your time of prayer with gratitude that you can be yourself in his presence.

Two. Consider Paul's advice to Timothy in the passage above. Paul, the world's most famous missionary, felt that he needed, and therefore displayed, God's "unlimited patience." Paul came to God without pretense: he knew he was a sinner. Why might someone want to avoid being vulnerable before God?

Three. Paul continues by exclaiming: *"Now to the King eternal, immortal, invisible, the only God, be honor and glory for ever and ever. Amen"* (1 Timothy 1:17). Read in the context of the previous verses, what do you think motivated such a shout of praise to God?

Taking the Spider Bite

When Keona was barely four, she found a spider on the floor. We have brown recluses in Missouri, so after squishing the spider soundly I proceeded to pick up the pair of pants I had laid out for Keona and run my arms through the legs.

"Mommy, what are you doing?" Keona asked.

I replied, "I'm running my hand through the pant legs so that if there are any other spiders, they'll bite me instead of biting you."

Keona's eyes welled up with tears. "You'll take the spider bite for me?"

"Of course, love," I whispered, realizing that this was a love-in-action picture for my daughter.

Then with tears rolling down her cheeks, she asked, "Mommy, what if I'm not strong enough to take the spider bite for my children? Will you take it for them too?"

Wrapping my arms around her, I answered, "As long as I have breath, I will do everything I can to take the spider bite."

It was a precious moment etched in my memory, but I hoped that the principle would last longer than a moment for my dear daughter.

Evidently it did. Not too long ago, Keona was telling me about a dream where she was attacked by a mean tiger. "That sounds scary," I empathized. "What happened?"

"Oh, it was okay," she replied calmly. "You took the tiger bite."

Yes indeed, while I have breath . . .

For Discussion and Reflective Journaling

Greater love has no one than this, that he lay down his life for his friends.

John 15:13

One. Whom would you "take the spider bite" for? Pray for each one as you list them by name.

Two. Who would "take the spider bite" for you? Thank God for each one as you list them by name.

Three. Jesus, ultimately, took sin's bite for us. Consider the following words and allow thanksgiving to well up in your heart for Christ's love and sacrifice:

> *When they hurled their insults at him, he did not retaliate; when he suffered, he made no threats. Instead, he entrusted himself to him who judges justly. He himself bore our sins in his body on the tree, so that we might die to sins and live for righteousness; by his wounds you have been healed.*
>
> *1 Peter 2:23–24*

Transported

One day my daughter's words suddenly transported me into Bible times. To be specific, I felt like I was listening in on Jesus' conversation with the Canaanite woman who asked him to have mercy on her and heal her troubled daughter:

> *He answered, "I was sent only to the lost sheep of Israel.*
> *. . . It is not right to take the children's bread and toss it*
> *to their dogs." "Yes, Lord," she said, "but even the dogs*
> *eat the crumbs that fall from their masters' table." Then*
> *Jesus answered, "Woman, you have great faith!*
> *Matthew 15:24–28*

I have heard reasonable sermons about the passage and have studied it personally as well. Frankly, it has always been a little difficult to process . . . until my daughter helped me.

Louie was twelve months old and his favorite "food" was a cheesy snack stick from a company that certainly lives on cruise ships based on how much they charge for sixteen pieces of snack food in a cute container . . . ANYWAY . . .

These were Louie's treats. They were made in a way that was easy for him to break down with his tiny teeth and gums. The rest of us had a wide variety of foods we could be nourished by, but Louie's choices at that time were very limited. Dear Keona knew this.

So one day, when I was feeding Louie, Keona asked, "Mommy, I know these are for Louie, but can I have the leftovers from Louie's snack if he throws them on the floor?"

There in my kitchen, I suddenly saw the Canaanite woman acknowledging that Jesus' earthly ministry was in many ways customized for the Jewish people. I saw her quietly but confidently asking for the "leftovers" to be made available for her, a Gentile.

Keona knew that I would give her anything in the fridge. She did not want to *take* Louie's food because she knew it was made especially for him. But if he discarded it, if he did not need or want it—could she feast on what he refused?

What did I do when faced with such a sensitive, wise, unashamed request? I opened the can and gave her fresh treats!

And I am still thinking about what all that means for me, a Gentile sinner saved by grace.

For Discussion and Reflective Journaling

Woman, you have great faith! Your request is granted.

Matthew 15:28

One. I doubt that this Canaanite mother thought of herself as possessing "*great faith.*" She simply loved her daughter and was desperate for help. Such love and desperation gave her a humble yet bold spirit. What prayers do you desperately need God to answer?

Two. Consider Hebrews 10:19–23 and spend a few moments reminding yourself that through Jesus you have access to God's throne room in prayer.

Three. Conclude your time by boldly bringing before Father God the needs that weigh most heavily on your heart.

An Eternal Exchange

The kingdom of heaven is like treasure hidden in a field,
which a man found and hid; and for joy over it he goes
and sells all that he has and buys that field.
                                        Matthew 13:44 NKJV

For joy—a man gladly sold everything he owned in this world for a treasure that had captured his heart.

Through this parable, Jesus illustrates what it is like to discover the kingdom of God: we willingly exchange whatever might be called gain in this world for the treasure of realizing God's loving leadership in our lives.

I remember the day joy led me to that life-size choice.

Years ago, I sincerely believed that there was no God. Without apology, I was an adamant Atheist.

Since I truly did not believe that God existed, I certainly did not expect to find him. But God found me. He was seeking me. On June 26, 1983, my existence was interrupted by Jesus—the God who pursues even those who deny him.

Joy seems too small a word to contain what it felt like to suddenly realize that God is, and that the God who is loved me. Though lost, I was not dense: I knew that laying down my broken life for such a God was like offering pennies to Fort Knox. But God was pleased with the offering of my life. He gladly received it. Amazing God. Amazing grace.

Decades later my soul still echoes the joy that the man in Jesus' parable knew. Without a moment's hesitation, today I would make the same life-size choice to exchange what will not remain for what cannot decay.[7]

For Discussion and Reflective Journaling

Again, the kingdom of heaven is like a merchant looking for fine pearls. When he found one of great value, he went away and sold everything he had and bought it.

Matthew 13:45–46

One. Jesus continued his teaching in Matthew 13 with a second illustration quoted above. Read these words carefully and ask God to reveal anything you have come to treasure more than him.

Two. Whether your entrance to the kingdom of God was a definite moment or a grace-filled process, retrace your first steps on God's path. Patiently recall the day or season you first discovered the priceless treasure of God's love.

Three. Over time, treasures can become dusty in our hearts. Comfort breeds casualness and casualness can breed carelessness. Conclude your time of reflection by inviting Jesus to help you value him and his salvation as the Great Treasure of your life.

Dear God . . .

Grant Me Wisdom
for This Journey

Lessons from the Road

On Driving Solo

Annual moves as a child . . . decades of summer road trips first as a daughter and now as a mother . . . parents who lived on the border of Mexico in Texas, and in-laws who lived on the border of Canada in North Dakota . . . ministry travel at home and abroad . . .

It would be frightening to know what percentage of my life has been spent suspended above four rubber circles. Over the miles, however, a few lessons have emerged for this road called life.

Lesson 1: Carpool

Whether to conserve the earth's resources, cut gas bills, enjoy company en route, or relish a break from always being in the driver's seat, carpooling has experienced a revival in our day.

Overall, carpooling is smart, but sharing space (in any context) comes with a cost.

A wise friend, Harvey Herman, once said, "It may be time, money, health, peace . . . but always remember: everything costs something."

Carpooling costs time (the larger the group, the longer and more complicated the ride) and autonomy (your schedule is not your own). Too much? Perhaps—until you consider the cost of driving solo: gas money from your pocket, miles on your vehicle, time finding parking, and—of greatest concern—no one nearby if you need help.

The parallels to a life of faith are obvious. Sharing space with others in a community of faith can be costly. But frankly, going it alone can be deadly.

This is a popular decision in our age. Many believe that we can be committed to God without being committed to the people of God. However, as you will hear me say every time I teach on mentoring, Jesus does not offer faith for independent study. Christianity is lived in the plural, not the singular.

Some choose to spiritually drive solo to protect themselves from more disappointment. The cost? Self-protection only weakens, and never strengthens, character.

Some spiritually opt out of the carpool to grant themselves more flexibility and freedom. The cost? We are more vulnerable to temptation when we distance ourselves from the community of faith, especially when that choice is made in the name of "freedom."

Though we may be perplexed by each other's preferences, though it is a guarantee that we will wound each other with careless words and insensitive ways, it is our shared, in-process humanity that anchors us to reality. The very imperfection of life-together grounds us and actually can protect us from floating off into spiritual strangeness and straying into spiritual danger.

Simply put: we are safer together than alone.

For Discussion and Reflective Journaling

Two are better than one,
    because they have a good return for their work:
If one falls down,
    his friend can help him up.
But pity the man who falls
    and has no one to help him up!
            Ecclesiastes 4:9–10

One. Read this Scripture slowly to yourself once again. These words were penned by Solomon, a man divinely gifted with wisdom. By name, identify the people in your life who are close enough, often enough, to know when you "*fall down*" and need "*help up.*"

Two. Some are energized by crowds, while others are renewed by solitude. Some share their lives easily, while others are innately cautious. How natural is it for you to share *life*—as opposed to just air on a Sunday morning—with other followers of Jesus?

Three. Spend a few minutes waiting on God, inviting him to reveal any way in which you are distancing yourself from others. Offer to him wounds or disappointments from past experiences with his people and ask him for the strength to stay close, even when it hurts.

Lessons from the Road

On Maps and Weariness

Lesson 2: Keep a Good Map Close By

Though familiar with people who are gifted with internal GPS, I am spatially (and woefully) disoriented.

For the skeptical, consider this: as a college student I lost my car at a mall in Austin, Texas. This fact can be attested to by my friend (whom I had driven to the mall), by my parents (whom I called from the mall even though they lived six hours away), and by the taxi driver (who drove me row by row through the entire parking lot until we found my wayward car). WHO KNEW that the store had exits onto two different levels?

Unfortunately, I have not grown out of this directional malady. After living in our house in Missouri for two years, I drove past the main road on the way home. An hour later it occurred to me that I had been driving a long time, but I still did not realize I was lost until my husband burst into concerned laughter when I called and asked, "Do we live near Mark Twain National Forest?"

More recently, a dear friend and I somehow managed to squeeze a three-hour drive into seven hours. I share these experiences to say this: maps are not optional for me; they are essential. Unlike instincts, maps do not change with our moods or alter with our circumstances.

Such is the power of God's Word. Though fresh every day, its ancient principles are certain and reliable; its age-old stories are relevant and inspiring. God's Word is a wise guide and ever true compass.

Keep it close.

Lesson 3: Pull Over when You Are Tired

Aging—for decades I thought this phenomenon was primarily reserved for the golden years of retirement. Then one day I turned thirty. Though nothing like the genetic displacement I suddenly experienced at the age of forty, thirty took me by surprise. Most notably, I reverted to my childhood need for a full night's sleep.

As a college student, I could string together two or even three study-all-nighters without even noticing. As young marrieds, Barry and I kept crazy college-student hours serving university students as campus ministers. But then, something changed.

Gone were the days of driving through the night and arriving at the destination fresh and sane. Gone was the confidence that we could just will our bodies to stay awake and our minds to stay alert.

With time, came perspective: life can be tiring. Any seasoned driver will affirm that when you are tired—for your sake and for the sake of others on the road—you need to pull over.

Is it time to pull over?

When weary, we must give ourselves permission to rest, to take a break, and to say, "No, thank you. Not now." Our culture has erroneously concluded that burning out for a good cause is a sign of commitment or even holiness.

But in the beginning, God blessed (and set the example for) work *and* rest. In his earthly ministry, Jesus taught on (and modeled) work *and* rest. They are interdependent: both are required to remain healthy.

For Discussion and Reflective Journaling

Your word is a lamp to my feet
and a light for my path.
Psalm 119:105

One. All of us wish we were more familiar with God's Word. But instead of regretting past lack, spend a few minutes brainstorming how you can incorporate God's Word more steadily into your future. Be creative and consider placing Bibles in rooms where you may have a few minutes to read, posting passages of Scripture on a window / on a nightstand / in a laundry room, winding down at night by reading a chapter instead of watching a show, listening to dramatic Bible readings on CD for errands in the car, the Psalms in song, and so on.

Two. On a scale of 1 (absolutely exhausted) to 10 (rested and refreshed), how would you rate yourself in these areas: (a) physically, (b) emotionally, (c) spiritually, (d) relationally, (e) occupationally (whether in the home or in the workplace)?

Three. How easy is it for you to give yourself permission to rest?

Four. Give yourself some advice. If you heard someone rate the areas in question two as you did, what would you encourage that person to do? In the words of Jesus, "*Go and do likewise*" (Luke 10:37).

Lessons from the Road

On Tune-ups and Choices

Lesson 4: Tune-ups Are Cheaper than Breakdowns

"It was probably nothing," I said to Barry, wondering why the car's brakes seemed sluggish as I pulled into the restaurant. Lacking confidence as a driver, I tried to dismiss my concerns but something lingered in my gut.

One week later, Barry was driving when he whispered, "Dear God," and gripped the steering wheel. Our brakes completely failed while we were driving down a steep hill in rush-hour traffic. Barry swerved into the empty oncoming lane to avoid rear-ending the long line of waiting cars at the red light. By the grace of God and my husband's level head, we crashed into the intersection without anyone suffering harm.

The policeman treated us like thrill-seeking graduate students until the driver of the tow truck tried to move our totaled car. "No brakes," he mouthed, and the policeman immediately softened. It was a miracle that everyone walked away without even a scratch.

I have often looked back on that day at the restaurant. Why did I not take my concerns more seriously? Yes, I knew little about cars. Yes, it had been raining. But additionally, I remember being worried about finances. We were newly married and living on love. But the tune-up would have been much cheaper than the crash, financially *and* emotionally.

With our vehicles and in our lives, when we ignore the need to attend to small things, we will eventually be immobilized by big things that are impossible to ignore.

A stop at the mechanic for the car, an appointment with the doctor for the ache, a consult with a trainer for the weight gain, a visit with a financial advisor for the budget, time with a counselor for the relationship, a long talk with a mentor for peace of mind . . .

Tune-ups can be lifesavers.

Lesson 5: Share the Road

"Share the road" signs normally alert motorists to the presence of bicyclists, but near my home, the phrase more often refers to the horse-drawn carriages of the Amish that grace several country roads here in the Ozarks. Encountering an Amish couple or family on the road is always a refreshing reminder for me of the beauty of simplicity as well as a reminder to remain alert for who or what might be around the corner.

Every choice in this road called life involves others. All decisions (and non-decisions) are felt by more than one soul. Those behind, beside, and even ahead of us are affected by our turns, detours, and distractions.

In reverse, it is certain that we too will be affected by others on the road. Their choices are not within our control, but our responses to their choices *are*.

None of us knows what lies around the next bend. But it is our responsibility to live in such a way that we do not intentionally cause harm.

For Discussion and Reflective Journaling

If it is possible, as far as it depends on you, live at peace with everyone.

Romans 12:18

One. Under Lesson 5 I wrote, "Those behind, beside, and even ahead of us are affected by our turns, detours, and distractions." Take a few moments to bring to mind the names and faces of those with whom you "share the road."

Two. Pray for each one with an awareness that your choices affect their lives.

Three. Reflecting on the encouragement in Lesson 4 to take time for tune-ups, talk with Father God about areas in your life that could benefit from wise counsel and professional assistance. For example, "Father, I'm not managing anger well in this situation. Bring to my mind someone who could help me process these recurring emotions."

Lessons from the Road

On Storms and Inches

Lesson 6: Drive Slower in Stormy Weather

Leah's hand gripped my tense arm. "I-think-I-see-a-TOR-NAAAA-DO!!!" she screamed.

Though we laugh retelling the story, in the moment we were all terrified. Well, Leah and I were terrified. Sarah was in the backseat wrestling with a map, oblivious to the pieces of road signs and furniture blowing across the highway.

My relationship with these two amazing women began with mentoring and quickly grew into lifelong friendship. They were traveling with me to a speaking engagement in Texas and, unbeknownst to us, we were driving straight into the path of three tornados just south of downtown Dallas.

"I think we missed our turn back there," Sarah offered pointing to the map.

My vision blurred by sheets of rain, and my heart pounding as I monitored the mounting winds, I shouted, "IS THERE ANYONE IN THE NEXT LANE?!"

"Why is everyone screaming?" Sarah asked, and then she looked up.

Though Leah is, indisputably, the queen, Sarah and I both have a good dose of drama running through our veins. All three of us prayer-shouted our way off the highway, onto the access road, and into the safety of a nearby building where we waited out the storm. An hour later we returned to the car and drove very slowly to the campground, entirely missing my first session but eventually arriving safely at our destination.

186

Tornados come in many different forms. The physical ones can tear up land and houses, but the emotional ones can tear up hearts and homes.

In darker, more turbulent times, we need to live more (not less) cautiously. Remaining alert is a must when it is hard to see. Wisdom invites us to slow down in such stormy seasons: to monitor our choice of surroundings, to guard against distractions, and to expend energy focusing on truth.

(And it always helps to ask a few dramatic, prayer-shouting friends to accompany you along the way.)

Lesson 7: Enjoy Every Inch of the Journey

Wherever we are, however we got here, there is something to appreciate and something to learn in this moment. Time is a gift. Another breath is not a given. In the end, my guess is that we all will mourn the energy we wasted daydreaming about "tomorrow" and rewinding "yesterday."

As you turn the last page in this book, I leave you with one of my soul's primary guiding principles:

Life is not about the scenery.

Life is all about the Company.

God is with us.

And his presence is enough.

For Discussion and Reflective Journaling

Finally, my brothers, rejoice in the Lord! It is no trouble for me to write the same things to you again, and it is a safeguard for you.

Philippians 3:1

One. If you currently find yourself within a storm, spend a few minutes reflecting on the following: (1) Do your chosen surroundings protect you or make you more vulnerable? (2) Are there distractions in your life that could be dangerous? (3) Are you expending energy focusing on truth? (4) Have you invited a few prayer-shouting friends to accompany you?

Two. Looking back over the last four devotionals, reorder these seven "lessons from the road" in terms of their importance and/or relevance for your journey currently. Slowly, pray over the "lessons" that are at the top of your list.

Three. Personally, I want to thank you for the time and attention you have invested in these devotionals. Please feel free to email me your thoughts and suggestions, just in case I write another devotional someday. You can reach me on my website at www.truthportraits. com or on facebook at truthportraits tribe.

Four. "Life is not about the scenery. Life is all about the Company. God is with us." Conclude in a time of thanksgiving for God's excellent company on this road called life.

Notes

1. Brother Lawrence, *The Practice of the Presence of God* (New Kensington, PA: Whitaker House, 1982), 81.
2. Ibid., 80–81.
3. Bridgid Herman, *Creative Prayer* (New York, NY: Cosimo Classics, 2007), 5.
4. When *Anonymous: Jesus' Hidden Years and Yours* was published, we had only two children. The "son" in this story is my eldest boy, Jonathan.
5. Richard Swenson, *Margin: Restoring Emotional, Physical, Financial, and Time Reserves to Overloaded Lives* (Colorado Springs: NavPress, 2004).
6. This devotional was written when my eldest son entered third grade in 2006.
7. Alicia's journey from Atheism to faith in Jesus is shared in *Finding an Unseen God: Reflections of a Former Atheist* (Grand Rapids: Bethany, 2009).

alicia britt chole

To connect with Alicia, hear her speak, learn more about her resources, or order the 7-week DVD Bible study for *Anonymous: Jesus' Hidden Years and Yours*, visit:

www.truthportraits.com
facebook: truthportraitstribe

"Alicia writes like she speaks and speaks like she writes: poetry that cuts to the heart."
- a twenty-something blogger

Alicia Britt Chole (uh-lee-shuh brit show-lee) speaks nationally to leaders, pastors, professionals, college students, women, and churches. All who have heard her agree: Alicia is an unusually disarming combination of realism and compassion, intellect and vulnerability, humor and art.

**two threads
one story
no fluff**

Creatively written, **Finding an Unseen God** blends Alicia's spiritual journey with her reflections on life and faith as a former Atheist.

```
M E A N I N G J F E A N H O H
P T S G N A K S C R W I B O T
Z E F L X G N O K I O G P X A
R N O I T S E U Q U N E V S P
J O U R N E Y L N Q D B M C L
E I T F N D E O N N E T S I L
G T C R B A I A K I R W F A S
D R A P A S M N A H Y E P S T
E U F B U E I H G T H K E C L
L T A L E H H M I L C A N I H
W H L R T D N L V A R O N E D
O I E C P F A I T H A G T N P
N U N S E E N J A F E S I C B
K Q I N R G O D W P S M K E H
```

REFLECTIONS OF A FORMER ATHEIST

"Simply put: *Anonymous* transformed me."

anonymous

Jesus' hidden years
and yours

alicia britt chole

These words have been repeated over and over by
leaders across the nation. *Anonymous* is stirring
a generation. Jesus' first three decades of life were
mostly hidden. However, with his life (and with ours),
it is critical that we not mistake unseen for unimportant.
Hidden years are unapplauded but not unproductive.
They are sacred spaces, to be rested in not rushed through
and most definitely never to be regretted.

In this personal, reflective book, Alicia helps us
recognize the riches that God grows in us during
uncelebrated seasons of our lives.

To learn more about the book and its reflective DVD study curriculum,
visit **www.truthportraits.com**.

Better together...

MOPS is here to come alongside you
during this season of early mothering to
give you the support and resources you
need to be a great mom.

Get connected today!

Mothers of Preschoolers

2370 S. Trenton Way, Denver CO 80231
888.910.MOPS • www.MOPS.org